MW00676889

THE *Taste* OF *Success*
RECIPES FROM HAWAI'I'S VIPS

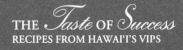

Rehabilitation Hospital of the Pacific Foundation
226 North Kuakini Street
Honolulu, Hawaii 96817
(808) 544-3301 Fax: (808) 544-3335

Published by
ISLAND HERITAGE
for the Rehabilitation Hospital of the Pacific Foundation

First Edition, First Printing - October 1995
ISBN# 0-89610-211-4

THE *Taste* OF *Success*

RECIPES FROM HAWAI'I'S VIPS

Proceeds to benefit the Rehabilitation Hospital of the Pacific

Ginger by Joyce Arizumi Pastels, 1994

"This program has enabled me to develop my creativity, which may have remained hidden."

Rebuilding Lives Together...

reflects the spirit of the Rehabilitation Hospital of the Pacific (REHAB). In many ways, our motto exemplifies the spirit of the islands as well as...people working together in harmony to help others.

REHAB appreciates the many people who work to help us fulfill our mission. Our first VIP cookbook, *The Taste of Success,* is not only a tribute to our supporters, but is another example of their aloha. The proceeds, after all, will help renovate REHAB's 42 year old building. We are grateful for the kokua of the community leaders who answered our request for recipes.

We would also like to recognize the artists from the Louis Vuitton Creative Arts Program at REHAB. Their original art works - created in spite of physical disabilities - grace the pages of this cookbook.

To the authors of these pages, our heartfelt thanks for sharing your special messages and most secret recipes. To you fans of good food who bought this cookbook, mahalo from REHAB for helping individuals with physical disabilities.

Bon appetite!

Michael W. Perry
Chairman of the Board
REHAB Foundation

Stuart T. K. Ho
Secretary/ Treasurer
REHAB Foundation

Onion by Keith Sasaki Watercolor, 1994

"Through art, I now have the confidence to be a participant in life, as opposed to a spectator."

Table of Contents

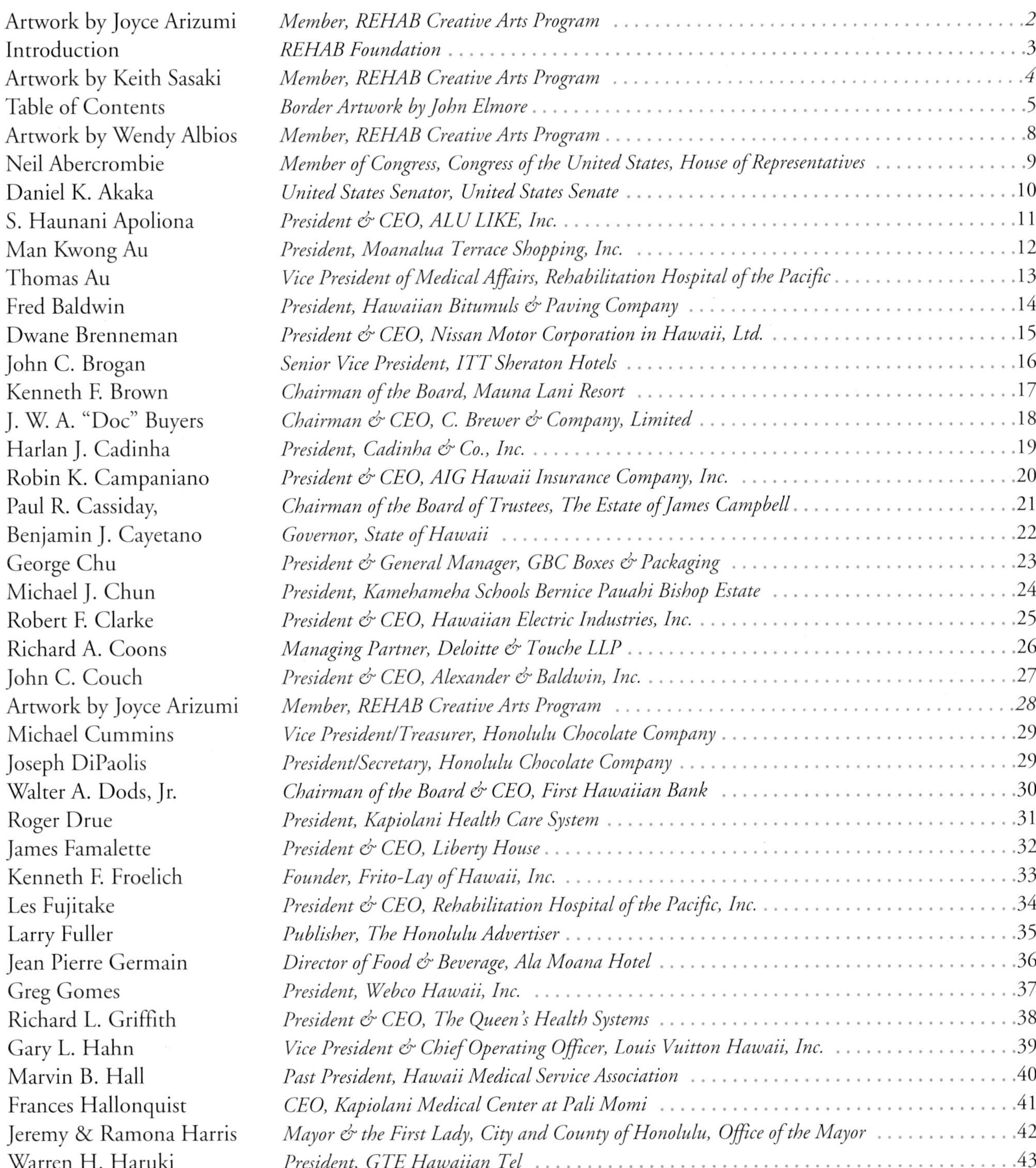

Table of Contents *continued*

Table of Contents *continued*

Hawaiian Dance by Wendy Albios — Pastels, 1994

"I've learned to see the world differently now."

NEIL ABERCROMBIE
1ST DISTRICT, HAWAII
REGIONAL WHIP

COMMITTEE ON
NATIONAL SECURITY
COMMITTEE ON
RESOURCES

Congress of the United States
House of Representatives
Washington, D.C. 20515

POTATO CHIP COOKIES

My favorite cookie recipe from my mother, Vera Abercrombie:

1/2 lbs.	Margarine (2 sticks)
1/2 cup	Sugar
dash	Vanilla
1 3/4 cup	Flour
1 1/4 cup	Potato chips (crushed)

Cream butter and sugar, add vanilla.
Add flour then add crushed potato chips.
Mix all together in one bowl.
Chill for awhile (1/2 hour) so dough can be handled.
Roll each piece into a ball.
Press down with a fork.
Bake for 13 to 15 min. at 350 degree. (Brown at the edge)
Sprinkle with confectionery sugar.

Neil Abercrombie

Neil Abercrombie
Member of Congress

ORIGINATED FROM:
☑ WASHINGTON OFFICE: 1233 LONGWORTH HOUSE OFFICE BUILDING, WASHINGTON, D.C. 20515 (202) 225-2726
☐ HOME OFFICE: ROOM 4104, 300 ALA MOANA BLVD., HONOLULU, HAWAII 96850 (808) 541-2570

DANIEL K. AKAKA
HAWAII

WASHINGTON OFFICE:
720 HART SENATE OFFICE
BUILDING
WASHINGTON, DC 20510
TELEPHONE: (202) 224-6361

HONOLULU OFFICE:
3104 PRINCE JONAH KUHIO
KALANIANAOLE FEDERAL BUILDING
P.O. BOX 50144
HONOLULU, HI 96850
TELEPHONE: (808) 522-8970

United States Senate
WASHINGTON, DC 20510-1103

MEMBER:
COMMITTEE ON ENERGY AND
NATURAL RESOURCES
COMMITTEE ON GOVERNMENTAL AFFAIRS
COMMITTEE ON INDIAN AFFAIRS
COMMITTEE ON VETERANS' AFFAIRS

March 20, 1995

Dear Friends of the REHAB Foundation:

It is my pleasure to submit a favorite recipe to be included in the Rehabilitation Hospital of the Pacific VIP Cookbook.

KOREAN CHICKEN

5-lb bag of chicken

Batter:
1/2 - 1 cup flour
1 Tbsp. salt

Sauce:
1 stalk green onion
1/2 cup shoyu
6 Tbsp. sugar
1 clove garlic, chopped
1 tsp. sesame oil
1 small red pepper (optional)

Salt chicken and let stand overnight. Roll chicken in flour and fry. After frying, dip in sauce and serve.

Aloha pumehana,

Daniel K. Akaka

DANIEL K. AKAKA
U.S. Senator

PRINTED ON RECYCLED PAPER

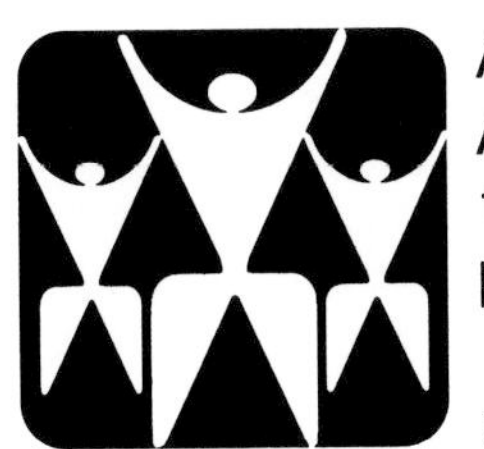

ALU LIKE, Inc.
Administrative Offices
1024 Māpunapuna Street
Honolulu, Hawai`i 96819-4417

Phone: (808) 836-8940 FAX: (808) 834-4702

E alu like mai kākou, e nā `ōiwi o Hawai`i
(Let us work together, natives of Hawai`i)

Like the Rehabilitation Hospital of the Pacific, **ALU LIKE, Inc.** is dedicated to rebuilding lives. Our mission, to kōkua Hawaiian natives who are committed to achieving their potential, is achieved when people work together to make themselves, their families and their communities healthy and whole. In today's society, culinary trends come and go. But at **ALU LIKE**, we have a recipe for healthy living that improves with age. It's easy, it's uplifting, and best of all, the more chefs in the kitchen, the better. Try it daily, as well as on special occasions. We think you'll love the results.

ALU LIKE

E alu like mai kākou	Let us work together
E nā ʻōiwi ō Hawaiʻi	Natives of Hawaiʻi
Nā pua maeʻole	The beautiful handsome descendants
E alu like mai kākou	Let us work together
E nā ʻōiwi ō Hawaiʻi	Natives of Hawaiʻi
Nā pua maeʻole	The descendants (flowers) that never fade
Nā pua maeʻole	The descendants (flowers) that never fade
I.	
E hana me ka ʻōiaʻiʻo	Let us work with sincerity
E hana me ka haʻahaʻa	Let us work with humility
E ʻōlelo pono kākou	Let us speak at all times with goodness/righteousness
E hana me ka ʻōiaʻiʻo	Let us work with sincerity
E hana me ka haʻahaʻa	Let us work with humility
E ʻōlelo pono kākou	Let us speak at all times with goodness/righteousness
E ʻōlelo pono kākou	Let us speak at all times with goodness/righteousness
(HUI)	
II.	
E nānā aku i ke kumu	Let us look to the source (of our strength)
E hoʻolohe mai	Let us listen (to that source)
E paʻa ka waha	Let us work not so much with the mouth
E hana me ka lima	Let us work more with the hands
E nānā aku i ke kumu	Let us look to the source (of our strength)
E hoʻolohe mai	Let us listen (to that source)
E paʻa ka waha	Let us work not so much with the mouth
E hana me ka lima	Let us work more with the hands
E paʻa ka waha	Let us work not so much with the mouth
E hana me ka lima	Let us work more with the hands

S. Haunani Apoliona, President/CEO

Moanalua Terrace Shopping, Inc.

MOANALUA SHOPPING CENTER

TELEPHONE 422-2434 P.O. BOX 618-D HONOLULU, HAWAII 96818

Salmon fixed this way has been favorite of my family since king salmon has been readily available. This is an fast and easy way to prepare salmon and most flavorful. The men can be the chefs while the women take care of the other courses.

ROSEMARY GRILLED SALMON

1 salmon filet about 4 pounds or a 4 pound whole fish split lengthwise.

8 to 10 sprigs of rosemary about width of the grill

MARINADE:

½ cup lime juice or white wine <u>or</u> combination of both
1 tsp. garlic, minced
Fresh chopped herbs, optional
Fresh ground pepper
2 Tbs.Oil

Mix the above in a flat pan and marinate salmon ½ hour or longer. Heat grill over medium heat. Wet rosemary and place 4 - 5 sprigs front to back across grill. Oil well if no rosemary sprigs are used. Sprinkle bits of rosemary on filet. Place cut side of filet down first. Grill about 5 minutes (allow ten minutes total per inch at thickest part.) Lift salmon and put on 5 more sprigs of fresh rosemary and put skin side down; grill another 5 minutes. Test for doneness; do not overcook.

Charred rosemary should be scraped off. Heat marinade and pour over fish. Garnish with rosemary or dill. Serve 6 - 8.

Man Kwong Au
President

THOMAS AU, M.D., INC.
KUAKINI MEDICAL PLAZA
321 NORTH KUAKINI STREET, SUITE 807
HONOLULU, HAWAII 96817

TELEPHONE (808) 521-3885

BASEBALL FRIED CHICKEN

1 1/2 pounds chicken thighs (cut in half)
2 tsp. sesame oil
1 Tbsp. shoyu
1 tsp. rice wine (optional)
1/2 tsp. salt
1/2 tsp. sugar
2 tsp. minced ginger
1 clove garlic, minced

Marinate the chicken with the above ingredients for 30 minutes then coat chicken pieces with the following mixture and fry.

Coating: Mix one egg and 1/4 cup cornstarch.

Sauce:
2 Tbsp. shoyu
1 Tbsp. sugar
2 tsp. sesame oil
1 clove garlic, minced
1/2 tsp. hot soy bean paste or chili sauce with garlic

Combine above ingredients in a small pot and heat until warm. Pour sauce over fried chicken and serve. Enjoy!

Thomas Au, M. D.

Hawaiian Bitumuls & Paving Compan

P.O. Box 2240, Honolulu, HI 96804 / Phone (808) 845-39

TIELLA
(Italian Zucchini Casserole)

This is my favorite recipe that comes from my Italian grandmother, Rachaela Posteraro. It is very easy to make, extremely healthy and even tastes better on day 2 or 3 reheated.

ENJOY!

INGREDIENTS: Preheat oven to 350°

4	Medium Potatoes, peeled and sliced into 1/8" slices
4-5	Medium Zucchini squash, sliced into 1/8" slices
2	Cloves Garlic, finely chopped
	Fresh Parsley
	Oregano
	Basil
	Salt & Pepper
	Parmesan cheese
1/2	Green Bell Pepper, cut into 3/8" wide strips
1	Large Can (28 oz.) Peeled Whole Tomatoes (save juice)
2	Tbsp. vegetable oil

PREPARATION:

1. Oil bottom and sides of 9" x 13" pyrex baking dish
2. Spread 1 clove chopped garlic into oil.
3. Build 3 consecutive layers as follows:
   - Potato slices
   - Zucchini slices
   - Cut/chunk 2-3 tomatoes / layer
   - Sprinkle Oregano (somewhat generously)
   - Sprinkle Basil (not so generously)
   - Salt & Pepper
   - Sprinkle Parmesan cheese ("not-a-too-much and not-a-too-little, but just-a-right!")
   - Finely cut and sprinkle fresh parsley

   START OVER WITH LAYER #2
4. When you finish layer #3, sprinkle second chopped garlic clove.
5. Pour leftover juice from tomato can over top layer "Zig-a-zag-a" style
6. Lay strips of green bell pepper across top evenly spaced.
7. Bake at 350 degrees for 1 hour and 15 minutes to 1 hour and 30 minutes. Fork test layers for doneness. Don't overcook. Tastes better second day warmed up as seasonings have marinated -- "Just like fine Italians!"

Fred Baldwin

Fred Baldwin
President

A Division of Dillingham Construction, A Majority Employee-Owned Company.

NISSAN MOTOR CORPORATION IN HAWAII, LTD.

DWANE BRENNEMAN
President & Chief Executive Officer

DB's DA'SSERT

Crust:

- 1/2 cup butter - melted
- 1 small pkg. pecans - chopped
- 1 cup flour
- 1/2 tsp. salt
- 1 tsp. baking soda
- 1/2 tsp. baking powder

Mix all ingredients together well. Press into greased square pan and bake at 425 for 20 minutes or until golden brown. Cool.

Filling:

- 1 8 oz. cream cheese - softened
- 1 cup powdered sugar
- 1 tsp. vanilla
- 1/2 of large container - Cool Whip

Spread filling on cooled crust.

Mix 1 large pkg. of instant chocolate pudding and spread on top of cream cheese topped crust. Frost with remaining Cool Whip and sprinkle with chopped pecans.

Refrigerate.

2880 Kilihau Street, Honolulu, Hawaii 96819
Telephone: (808) 836-0888

John C. Brogan
SENIOR VICE PRESIDENT
AREA DIRECTOR OF OPERATIONS, HAWAII

Visitors and Kamaainas alike have flocked to the Royal Hawaiian Hotel's Surf Room since 1927 to taste the hotel's famous Macadamia Nut Cream Pie, with its smooth taste of coffee liqueur.

MACADAMIA NUT CREAM PIE

Makes one 9-inch pie

Royal Hawaiian Hotel
Honolulu, Hawaii

1 9-inch Rich Pastry Shall
1/2 cup sugar
4 tablespoons sifted cornstarch
1/2 teaspoon salt
2 cups milk
4 egg yolks, lightly beaten
1 tablespoon butter
2 tablespoons Kahlua Liqueur
3/4 cup (4 ounces) macadamia nuts
2 cups whipped cream

Prepare and bake Rich Pastry Shell according to the recipe. Combine the sugar, cornstarch, and salt in top of a double broiler. Slowly add milk, stirring constantly. Place over gently boiling water and cook 10-15 minutes. Stir constantly until mixture thickens to a loose custard consistency. Blend 1/2 cup of the hot sugar mixture into the beaten egg yolks, 1 tablespoon at a time. Slowly pour and beat the warm egg mixture back into the remaining sugar mixture. Continue cooking 3-5 minutes, until the custard is quite thick. Add the butter; cool to room temperature. When cool, stir in the Kahlua Liqueur and all but 1 tablespoon of the chopped nuts. Fold in 1 cup whipped cream. Fill the baked pastry shell; garnish with the remaining whipped cream and reserved nuts. Chill.

RICH PASTRY SHELL

Makes one 9-inch pie shell

2 cups all-purpose flour
Dash of salt
1/4 cup butter, softened
2 egg yolks, lightly beaten
1 tablespoons water

Place flour and salt in a large bowl. Make a well in the center and put into it the butter, yolks, and water. Using your fingertips, gradually pull in the flour. Mix until all ingredients are well combined and dough forms a ball. Cover. Chill several hours before using.

Preheat oven to 450 degrees. Roll our the dough and place in a 9-inch pie pan. Prick the bottom several times with a fork. Bake 12-15 minutes, or until crust is crisp but not brown.

John C. Brogan

2155 KALAKAUA AVENUE, SUITE 300, HONOLULU, HAWAII 96815
PHONE: (808) 921-4040 FAX: (808) 923-0851

MAUNA LANI RESORT

BARBECUED BUTTERFLIED LAMB

Leg of Lamb, deboned and butterflied
3/4 cup teriyaki sauce
1/2 cup tomato puree
1 can (8 oz.) crushed pineapple, undrained
2 Tbsp. honey
1 tsp. ground ginger
1 lemon, sliced

Combine teriyaki, puree, pineapple, honey, ginger and lemon slices.

Pour over lamb and marinate several hours or overnight.

Place lamb fat side up under broiler. Broil six (6) inches from heat until desired degree of doneness. Baste with marinate and turn once.

Kenneth F. Brown
KENNETH F. BROWN
Chairman of the Board

P.O. Box 4959 • Kohala Coast • Island of Hawaii 96743-4959
Telephone: (808) 885-6677 • TELEX: 752449 • FAX: (808) 885-6375

C. BREWER AND COMPANY, LIMITED

P. O. Box 1826
Honolulu, Hawaii 96805
Telephone (808) 544-6200
FAX (808) 544-6182

J. W. A. BUYERS
Chairman
Chief Executive Officer

One of the most unique institutions in Hawaii is the Rehabilitation Hospital of the Pacific, which has always had my unqualified support. The Board of Directors of REHAB is outstanding in every respect, and they are deeply concerned about improving the health and mobility of our community. Therefore, it is only fitting that I provide a healthful and scrumptious recipe for this new cookbook, which is "Pineapple Carrot Cake Macadamia" from my daughter's publication, *The Marvelous Macadamia Nut*. This is a delicious dessert and it is easy to make and wonderful to consume. Bon appetit!

Pineapple Carrot Cake Macadamia

1 ½ cups vegetable oil
2 cups granulated sugar
4 eggs
2 cups flour
1 tsp. cinnamon
2 tsp. baking soda
1 tsp. salt
3 cups grated carrots
1 cup macadamia nut bits
8-oz. can crushed pineapple, drained

Preheat the oven to 350 degrees. Grease a 10-inch tube pan.

Blend together the oil, sugar and eggs and beat well. Sift together the flour, cinnamon, baking soda and salt in a separate bowl and add to the egg mixture. Stir thoroughly. Fold in the grated carrots, macadamias and pineapple and pour the batter into the prepared pan.

Bake in the preheated oven for 1 hour, or until a cake tester inserted in the center comes out clean. Cool the cake in the pan. When cold, remove from the pan and frost with Pineapple Cream Cheese Icing (below).

Pineapple Cream Cheese Icing

8-oz. package cream cheese, softened
8-oz. can crushed pineapple, drained

Beat together the cream cheese and crushed pineapple, using an electric mixer, until light and fluffy. Serves 10-12

J. W. A. Buyers
Chef Plagiarize

CADINHA & CO., INC.
REGISTERED INVESTMENT ADVISERS
PIONEER PLAZA
900 FORT STREET MALL, SUITE 1240
HONOLULU, HAWAII 96813
TELEPHONE: (808) 523-9488
FACSIMILE: (808) 526-9725

LAYERED TACO SPREAD

1 16-ounce can refried beans
1/2 cup taco sauce
3/4 cup shredded sharp natural cheddar cheese (3 ounces)
1 8-ounce package cream cheese, softened
1/4 cup dairy sour cream
3 Tbsp. mayonnaise
1/4 tsp. garlic powder
1 large avocado, seeded and peeled
1 medium onion, cut up
1 Tbsp. lemon juice
1/2 cup sliced pitted ripe olives
1/2 cups sliced green onions
Tortilla Chips

In 3-cup bowl, stir together refried beans, taco sauce, and several dashes bottled hot pepper sauce, if desired. Spread the refried bean mixture evenly on bottom and sides of 13 x 9 x 2 pan. Sprinkle half of the shredded cheese over the bean layer.

In small mixing bowl combine the cream cheese, sour cream, mayonnaise and garlic powder; beat with an electric mixer on medium speed until smooth. Spread the cream cheese mixture evenly over the cheese.

Cut avocado into small pieces. In a blender add avocado, onion and lemon juice and blend until combined. Spread the avocado mixture evenly over the cream cheese layer.

Sprinkle avocado layer with chopped tomato, sliced olives, sliced green onions and remaining cheese.

Chill for four hours. Serve with tortilla chips.

Harlan J. Cadinha
President

AIG Hawaii Insurance Company, Inc.
Six Waterfront Plaza • Third Floor • 500 Ala Moana Boulevard
Honolulu, Hawaii 96813 • (808) 545-1650

Steamed Black Bean Opakapaka

This is an easy, foolproof recipe which even the occasional cook like me can manage. It's healthy, it's easy, and those who taste it will wonder how you ever managed the time to prepare such a delightful dish!

One 2-3 lb. Opakapaka (ehu, onaga or uku will also work well)
Hawaiian salt
4 cloves fresh garlic - grated
2 Tbsp. fresh ginger - grated
1/2 cup black beans - rinsed and slightly mashed
6 large, pickled scallions - minced
1/2 cup green onion - diced
1 bunch Chinese parsley - chopped

1/3 cup shoyu
1 Tbsp. brown sugar
2 Tbsp. mirin
(These three ingredients should be mixed together.)

3/4 cup peanut oil
1 Tbsp. sesame oil
(Both these ingredients should be mixed and heated, very hot .)

Clean fish and lightly sprinkle with Hawaiian salt, in and out. Place fish in refrigerator for approximately 2-3 hours.

Spread garlic, ginger, black beans and scallions evenly over the fish, and inside fish, if desired. Place fish in steamer, steam about 8 minutes per pound.

Pour shoyu/brown sugar/mirin mixture over cooked fish. Sprinkle with green onions, then pour hot oil mixture (sizzling) over fish. Spread chopped Chinese parsley on fish and serve.

Robin K. Campaniano
President & Chief Executive Officer

PASTA SAUCE
(Low Fat)

1-1/2 cup non-fat cottage cheese or low fat ricotta

1/4 cup grated parmesan

1/2 cup fresh basil or coriander (leaves only)

1/2 cup chopped parsley leaves

4 cloves minced garlic

2 Tbsp. to 1/2 cup skim milk or non-fat yogurt

Put into food processor. Serve cold over pasta of your choice. Sauce can be heated.

Paul R. Cassiday

Paul R. Cassiday
Chairman, Board of Trustees

1001 Kamokila Boulevard, Kapolei, Hawaii 96707 Phone (808) 674-6674 Facsimile (808) 674-3111

EXECUTIVE CHAMBERS

HONOLULU

BENJAMIN J. CAYETANO
GOVERNOR

Oxtail Soup

2 1/2 lbs.	Oxtail pieces
1	46oz. can Swanson's Chicken Broth plus 2 cups of water
3 cups	Water
1 tsp.	Salt
1	Medium round onion, minced
1	Rib celery, minced
1"	Piece fresh ginger root, peeled and lightly pounded
1 tbsp.	Ginger, grated
1	Piece star anise
1	Package raw shelled peanuts (approximately 2 ozs.)
1 cup	Blanched mustard cabbage

Trim and discard excess fat from oxtails. Set aside.

Bring 3 cups of water to a boil in 6 qt. pot, add 1 tsp. salt.

Add oxtails to boiling salted water and boil for 2 minutes.

Drain oxtails in colander.

Return oxtails to pot adding chicken broth, 2 cups water, onion, celery, star anise, 1" piece of ginger and peanuts.

Bring to a boil, reduce heat to simmer, cover, and cook over low heat for approximately 2 hours or till tender.

Correct seasoning.

Serve with mustard cabbage, garnish with chinese parsley and grated ginger.

Benjamin J. Cayetano
Governor
State of Hawaii

4478 MALAAI STREET
HONOLULU, HAWAII 96818

GBC
BOXES & PACKAGING

TELEPHONE: (808) 423-4111
FAX: (808) 423-7662

1 lb. Butter
1-1/2 Cup Sugar
1 Egg
4-1/2 Cups Flour
2 Cups Rice Krispies
3/4 Cup Coconut
1/2 Cup Chopped Nuts
1 Tsp Vanilla

Cream the butter and sugar
Add egg,vanilla, flour,coconut, rice krispies, and nuts.

Drop by teaspoon on cookie sheet and press each dough with a fork

Bake 350° for 20 minutes

George Chu
President & General Manager

KAMEHAMEHA SCHOOLS BERNICE PAUAHI BISHOP ESTATE

OFFICE OF THE PRESIDENT
EDUCATION GROUP
2010 PRINCESS DRIVE HONOLULU, HAWAI'I 96817-1598
TELEPHONE 808 842-8231 FAX 808 842-8411

In an attempt to cut back on red meat, this has become one of our Favorites:

TOFU PATTIES

Drain: 1 block firm tofu

Mix with:
1 egg, beaten
1 tsp. lemon juice
1/2 tsp. salt
2 oz. fresh mushrooms, sliced
dash of salt
1/2 cup green onions
1/2 cup fresh parsley, chopped
1/2 cup water chestnuts, chopped
oyster sauce to taste
6 oz. fish cake or 1 can crabmeat
4 Tbsp. panko

Make into patties and fry until browned. 5 minutes each.

Dr. Michael J. Chun, President

HAWAIIAN ELECTRIC INDUSTRIES, INC. • PO BOX 730 • HONOLULU, HI 96808-0730

Robert F. Clarke
President and
Chief Executive Officer

I like to grill and don't have any real "recipes." It's a team effort when we have company -- my wife does the prepping and I cook on the grill. This is one of our favorite menus.

Grilled Pork Loin

6 Tbsp. kosher salt
10 Tbsp. sugar
12 whole black peppercorns
6 whole cloves
3 bay leaves
3-4 sprigs fresh thyme
1 boneless pork loin, 2 to 2 1/2 pounds, well trimmed

Prepare pork two to three days before you want to serve it. Dissolve salt and sugar in warm water in a non-reactive pan or bowl. Add remaining ingredients and the pork loin. Add enough tap water to cover the pork loin. Cover with plastic wrap and refrigerate for two to three days.

Remove the pork from the brine and discard brine. Grill pork loin over moderate coals for about 40 minutes, turning occasionally. Check temperature: when pork reaches 150 degrees, remove from grill and let rest for 10 to 15 minutes.
Or, roast pork loin in oven at 325 degrees for about an hour or until temperature registers at 150 degrees.

Slice into 1/4 inch pieces and serve. Accompany with roasted vegetable salad and grilled bread.

Roasted Vegetable Salad

2 large zucchini
4 long eggplant
2 red peppers
2 Maui onions
2 bunches green onions
8 ripe tomatoes, preferably Roma
1 pound asparagus
Olive oil
Kosher salt
Balsamic vinegar
Freshly ground black pepper

Prepare vegetables for the grill. Slice zucchini and eggplant lengthwise into pieces about 1/4 to 1/2 inch thick. Sprinkle eggplant slices with salt and set aside for 30 minutes to remove bitterness. Rinse and pat dry.

Quarter the red peppers; remove stem and seeds. Slice Maui onions into 1/4 to 1/2 inch thick slices. Wash and trim green onions. Slice tomatoes into thick pieces. Break asparagus at bottoms. Thread onto bamboo skewers.

Drizzle vegetables with good quality olive oil and place on grill over hot coals. Sprinkle lightly with kosher salt. Cook each vegetable until tender; do not overcook. As you turn vegetables, brush with a little more olive oil. Place all vegetables on a platter.

While still warm, cut vegetables into bite sized pieces and place in a salad bowl. Drizzle with balsamic vinegar to balance the olive oil; season with salt and pepper. Toss well and serve.

Grilled Bread

Slice a crusty loaf of bread into 1/2 inch thick pieces. Toast slices on the grill for just a minute on each side. Bread should be toasted and heated through. Drizzle with olive oil and rub with a clove of garlic. Serve immediately.

Bob Clarke

Robert F. Clarke
President and Chief Executive Officer

Suite 1200
1132 Bishop Street
Honolulu, Hawaii 96813-2870

Telephone: (808) 543-0700
Facsimile: (808) 526-0225

We generally throw back salmon under 28", but this recipe is OK for <u>any</u> size fish!

DELOITTE & TOUCHE FISH CAMP SALMON

Rinse a whole, cleaned **salmon** (sans head) and paper towel dry. Lay it on two or three big pieces of heavy duty foil.

Use **garlic**, **salt** and **pepper** inside and out, then rub the skin with **olive oil** to prevent sticking.

Add water to a **package of hollandaise** sauce according to directions, stir in **1 teaspoon dried parsley, 1 teaspoon dill** and pour into and over fish.

Slice an **onion** and **lemon** and lay on top of fish.

Wrap tightly in foil and barbeque or bake 10 to 20 minutes per side depending on size or until a toothpick easily penetrates the thickest part.

8 oz. per serving.

Richard A. Coons

Deloitte Touche
Tohmatsu
International

JOHN C. COUCH
President and
Chief Executive Officer

My sweet tooth? You could say it is part of the job!

The pure white, golden brown and dark brown sugars refined by California and Hawaiian Sugar Company -- familiar to shoppers as C&H Sugar -- are made from thousands of green-growing acres of Hawaii's sugarcane, and nearly a third of it is grown by Alexander & Baldwin companies.

Pure energy is what you get from pure cane sugar and the healthy portion of C&H Cane Golden Brown Sugar in this recipe help make these Coconut Chews the best you can sink your sweet tooth into! They are a favorite at C&H company luncheons. Enjoy.

C&H Coconut Chews

Crust:
- 1/4 cup packed C&H Cane Golden Brown Sugar
- 1/2 cup (1 stick) butter or margarine, softened
- 2 cups all purpose flour
- 1/8 teaspoon salt

Filling:
- 3 cups packed C&H Cane Golden Brown Sugar
- 1-1/2 cups chopped nuts
- 1-1/2 cups flaked coconut
- 4 eggs, beaten
- 4 teaspoons vanilla

Preparation: Preheat oven to 350 degrees. Grease 13" x 9" x 2" baking dish.

Crust: In medium bowl using pastry blender or two knives, blend 1/4 cup sugar, butter, flour and salt until crumbly. Press mixture into baking dish.
Bake 20 minutes. Remove from oven to add filling.

Filling: In large bowl, combine remaining ingredients; spread on crust.
Bake 30 minutes or until center is firm.

Cool in pan; cut into bars. Makes 3 dozen.

John C. Couch

822 BISHOP STREET • P.O. BOX 3440 • HONOLULU, HAWAII 96801-3440 • TELEPHONE (808) 525-8487 • FAX (808) 525-6616

Strawberry Short Cake by Joyce Arizumi Oil, 1994

"Painting has been a satisfying and fun way of unlocking my creativity!"

HONOLULU CHOCOLATE COMPANY
1200 Ala Moana Boulevard
Honolulu, Hawaii 96814

Honolulu Chocolate's Favorite Recipe

CHOCOLATE TRUFFLES

2/3 cup heavy cream
1/4 cup unsalted butter, softened
7 ounces bittersweet chocolate
1 cup cocoa powder

In a saucepan over low heat, bring cream to a boil. Chop chocolate finely and combine with hot cream, stirring until melted and smooth. Stir in butter and blend well. Chill in refrigerator 1 - 2 hours. Place cocoa in a shallow pan. Using teaspoons, form small balls of chocolate mixture and roll in cocoa. Store in refrigerator.

Yield: 50 - 60 truffles

Joseph DiPaolis
President / Secretary

Michael Cummins
Vice President / Treasurer

P.O. Box 3200, Honolulu, Hawaii 96847

Walter A. Dods, Jr.
Chairman of the Board
and Chief Executive Officer

February 17, 1995

As a past director and long-time supporter of the Rehabilitation Hospital of the Pacific, I am keenly aware of the facility's good works and extensive healing that goes on there. They cannot do everything, however. Take the common cold. (Most of us would love to.) If you're feeling a little bit under the weather, try the wonder remedy that my Mom always gave to me: a great big bowl of Portuguese Bean Soup. Enjoy, but be careful. This "remedy" has been known to become habit forming.

Portuguese Bean Soup

2 pcs ham hock
1 tsp olive oil
1 cup carrots (diced)
1 cup round onions (diced)
1 cup celery (diced)
2 tbs fresh chopped parsley
6 pcs fresh garlic minced
4 cups fresh tomatoes chopped
2 pcs bay leaf
1 tbs thyme leaf
2 cups portuguese sausage chopped
1 can tomato paste (6 oz.)
Pinch of saffron (optional)
Salt & pepper to taste
2 cans kidney beans (15-1/2 oz)

In two gallons of water, boil ham hock, any leftover vegetables, bay leaf, thyme and saffron.

In another large pot, on medium heat, add olive oil then cook portuguese sausage until brown. Next add carrots, round onions, celery and garlic. Strain ham hock broth into second pot, adding the remaining ingredients. Salt and pepper to taste.

Optional, but so "ono": cabbage, macaroni and ham hock meat. You may thicken, if needed, with flour water.

WALTER A. DODS, JR.

KAPIOLANI HEALTH CARE SYSTEM

...for all you paniolos out there, here is a recipe handed down over the years from an original Oregon Trail chuckwagon cook named Emma Bear.

Served across the West for a 100 years, Hawaiians will appreciate the "campfire nature" of these beans!

EMMA'S BEANS

1 lb. hamburger
1 onion, chopped
1 green pepper, chopped
1 8-oz. can tomato sauce
1 large can pork-and-beans
2 dashes vinegar
2 Tbsp. brown sugar
Salt & pepper to taste

Brown hamburger lightly.
Add onion and green pepper.
Add remaining ingredients.
Turn into casserole dish.
Bake 400 degrees for
30 minutes, without cover.

Roger

Roger Drue
President

Artesian Plaza • 5th Fl. • 1907 South Beretania Street • Honolulu, Hawaii 96826 • Telephone (808) 973-3400 • FAX (808) 973-3474

EXECUTIVE
OFFICE

ITALIAN BISCUITS

Ingredients

2 cups of sugar
1/2 pound of butter
3 eggs beaten
1 pound of ricotta cheese
1 teaspoon of vanilla
4 cups of flour (sifting optional)
1 teaspoon of baking soda
1 teaspoon of salt
1 box of powdered sugar and 1 stick of butter for icing

Directions

Cream butter and sugar, add eggs, ricotta and vanilla then add baking soda, salt and flour. Drop by teaspoon on an ungreased cookie sheet. Bake at 350 degrees for approximately 15 minutes. Bottom of cookies should be a very, very light brown, don't over cook.

Icing cookies - If Christmas holidays, separate icing into 2 bowls. Add red and green food coloring, etc....

For icing, mix powdered sugar, butter and milk. (Add enough to make icing spreadable.)

James Famalette
President and
Chief Executive Officer

P.O. BOX 2690 • HONOLULU, HAWAII 96845 • (808)945-5500 • FAX (808)945-5571

Frito-Lay of Hawaii, Inc.

Ken Twelich
Founder

SUPER NACHOS - 90'S VERSION

1 Bag 14 ½ oz. Frito-Lay Brand BAKED TOSTITOS

1 ½ cups each Shredded Cheddar cheese & Monterey Jack cheese

1 cup Frito-Lay Brand TOSTITOS SALSA (fat free)

½ cup Jalapenos, sliced

½ cup Tomatoes, diced

1/4 cup Ripe Olives, sliced

Garnishes: Salsa, sour cream, sliced onion, guacamole

Spread chips out on a microwave proof platter.
Sprinkle with cheeses.
Microwave 1 or 2 minutes until the cheese melts.
Spoon on the 1 cup Salsa: top with remaining ingredients.
Garnish as desired.

99-1260 IWAENA STREET • AIEA, HAWAII 96701 • TELEPHONE: (808) 487-1515 • FAX: ADMIN. (808) 484-0437 SALES (808) 484-0484

REHAB *Rebuilding Lives Together*

Rehabilitation Hospital of the Pacific • 226 North Kuakini Street • Honolulu, HI 96817 • Telephone: (808) 531-3511 • FAX: 544-3335

Mahalo to my fellow colleagues, who share the pages in this cookbook with me. Their support and recipes helps us raise the necessary funds to upgrade our hospital and continue our proud service record as the resource for rehabilitation medicine in Hawaii and the Pacific. Below is my contribution from the Fujitake family, to you. Enjoy!

Fruit Cream Tarts

12 baked tart shells
1/4 cup sugar
2 Tbsp. cornstarch
1/4 tsp. salt
1 cup milk
1 egg (slightly beaten)
1 tsp. vanilla extract
1/2 cup heavy or whipping cream (whipped)
Strawberries (whole or sliced), blueberries, peach slices, mandarin orange sections (drained), or sliced kiwi fruit
12 baked tart shells

1. In 2-quart saucepan, mix sugar, cornstarch and salt; stir in milk until smooth. Over medium heat, cook, stirring until mixture boils; boil 1 minute.

2. In a small bowl, beat egg slightly, then slowly stir in a small amount of the hot milk mixture.

3. Slowly pour egg mixture into sauce, stirring rapidly to prevent lumping. Cook, stirring, until thickened (do not boil).

4. Cover with waxed paper and refrigerate. When the custard is cold (after about 40 minutes), stir in vanilla extract; then with wire whisk, fold in whipped cream.

5. Spoon custard into baked tart shells. Top with fruit.

Optional - Melt 1 cup currant jelly and 1 tablespoon water in a 1-quart saucepan; cool slightly then spoon over fruit. Refrigerate until jelly sets.

Les Fujitake
President & CEO

The Honolulu Advertiser

LARRY FULLER
Publisher

Established 1856

STUFFED JUMBO SHELLS

1 32-oz. jar spaghetti sauce
3/4 tsp. cinnamon
1 package jumbo pasta shells (20-22 shells)
3 cups (24 ounces) no fat ricotta cheese
6 oz. shredded no-fat mozzarella cheese
1 egg
3/4 cup golden raisins
1/2 cup chopped walnuts
1/2 cup chopped dried apricots
1 tsp. sugar
1/4 tsp. freshly grated nutmeg

Cook pasta according to package direction. Drain. Rinse with cold water.

Heat sauce. Stir in cinnamon.
Spoon 1 cup sauce into bottom of shallow baking dish.
Mix remaining ingredients.
Stuff mixture into shells.
Arrange shells in single layer on top of sauce.
Cover and bake at 350 degrees for 30 minutes.
Serve with rest of heated sauce.

6-8 servings.

Larry Fuller
Publisher

Published by Gannett Pacific
Post Office Box 3110, Honolulu 96802 • (808) / 525-7474 FAX: (808) 525-8685

ALA MOANA HOTEL
HONOLULU, HAWAII

FRESH TOMATO SAUCE
also known as Marinara Sauce

1	#10 can of crushed plum tomatoes
4	large onions
12	cloves of garlic
1	cup olive oil
4	bay leaves
	salt - to taste
	fresh ground white pepper - to taste
1	cup fresh chopped basil
	fresh rosemary
½	bottle of white wine
½	cup sugar

1. Finely dice the onions. Use a Cuisinart if you have one.

2. Crush the 12 cloves of garlic with the flat side of a knife blade and chop coarsely.

3 In a saucepan, heat the olive oil, when hot but not too hot, add the onions and stir for a few minutes until transculent.

4. Add the can of crushed plum tomatoes and garlic. Rinse can of tomato with white wine and add to mixture, then add sugar, rosemary and bay leaves.

5. Stir well and add salt and pepper to taste. Use only fresh ground white pepper. Stir well and let cook for half an hour.

6. Then add the basil (finely chopped to the equivalent of 1 cup) and let cook for another half hour, stirring every 10 minutes.

7. Refrigerate in a glass jar until ready to use with your favorite pasta. May be kept for several months.

The secret to this recipe is not to use dry herbs.

JEAN PIERRE GERMAIN
Director of Food & Beverage

410 Atkinson Drive • Honolulu • Hawaii • 96814-4722 • Phone: (808) 955-4811 • Fax: (808) 947-7338 • Telex: (808) 743-0350

OFFICE OF THE PRESIDENT

Serving beautiful Hawaii

Lite and simple but so good. Keep copies of recipe handy because people will beg for it.

FOUR LAYER DELIGHT

1ST LAYER:

1-1/4 cups flour
1 block plus 2 Tbsp. margarine or butter at room temperature
1/2 cup chopped nuts

Hand mix in large bowl until crumbly. Press into 9" x 13" pan. Bake at 375 degrees for 15 minutes and let cool before adding second layer.

2ND LAYER:

2 cups cool whip
2 cups powdered confectioner sugar
16 oz cream cheese at room temperature

Blend together and spread over 1st layer.

3RD LAYER:

2 boxes (3.4 oz) jello vanilla instant pudding
3 cups cold milk

Mix and spread over 2nd layer.

4TH LAYER: Top with cool whip and chill.

Just before serving, top with fresh sliced bananas.

Greg

GREG GOMES

2840 Mokumoa Street, Honolulu, Hawaii 96819 Phone: (808) 839-4551 ext. 211 Fax: (808) 834-3350

THE QUEEN'S HEALTH SYSTEMS

201 Merchant Street, Suite 2450 • Honolulu, Hawaii 96813 • PH: 808 532-6100 • FAX: 808 532-6118

Who says healthy recipes have to be dull? Here's a red snapper recipe from Mexico that can be made with almost any island fish. It will knock your socks off!

Red Snapper Vera Cruz

(Serves 4)

Ingredients:

4 six oz. red snapper fillets
3 Tbsp. fresh lime juice to taste
salt & pepper to taste
1-1/2 lbs. fresh tomatoes
2 cloves garlic
4 Tbsp. stuffed green olives
1 tsp. capers
2 Tbsp. jalapeno pepper or similar chili
1/2 tsp. dried oregano
1 small Maui onion

Preparation:

1. Place the fillets in a lightly oiled baking pan. Drizzle with lime juice. Salt & pepper to taste. Cover and refrigerate while preparing the remaining ingredients.

2. Seed and chop the tomatoes into large chunks. Peel and mince the garlic. Slice the olives. Wash the peppers, then remove the stem, seeds and inner membranes. Mince or finely chop the remaining pulp.

3. Combine the tomatoes, garlic, olives, capers, peppers and oregano in a small bowl. Mix well, then spoon on top of the lime marinated fillets.

4. Thinly slice the onions and arrange over the fish. Bake in a 400-degree F. oven about 15 to 20 minutes or until the fish flakes easily.

5. Place fillets on serving plate and top with the vegetable sauce from the baking dish.

Richard L. Griffith

Richard L. Griffith
President & CEO
The Queen's Health Systems

MAISON FONDEE EN 1854

LOUIS VUITTON HAWAII
2255 KUHIO AVENUE, #1400
HONOLULU, HAWAII 96815
TEL: (808) 924-1066
FAX: (808) 923-2585

Taste Great Salad

Here's a recipe that's low in fat content, full of things that are good for you and it tastes great.

3 cups broccoli (cut up small, include small stems)
1 cup grated carrots
1 cup golden raisins
1/2 cup honey roasted nuts
1/4 cup green onion

Mix all ingredients in a bowl with a lid.

<u>Dressing</u>

1 cup non fat miracle whip
1/2 cup sugar
1/4 cup vinegar (white)
salt & pepper to taste

Mix all ingredients together, if too sour, add sugar to taste. Pour dressing over, toss & refrigerate for at least 2 hours tossing a couple times.

Will keep refrigerated for 2 days.

This will make the salad your favorite element of the meal.

Gary L. Hahn
Vice President & COO

An Independent Licensee of the Blue Cross and Blue Shield Association

Marvin B. Hall
President
(808) 944-3578

An easy, quick, delicious, reasonably low-fat, and low-calorie meal.

CHICKEN AND BISCUITS

1 medium onion, chopped
1 Tbsp. margarine (or butter)
1/4 cup flour
1/4 tsp. each salt and pepper
3-1/2 cups low-fat milk
1 lb. diced, cooked chicken breast
1 package frozen peas and carrots, cooked
  (amount can be adjusted to taste)
1 tsp. each dried sage and thyme
  (1 tsp. dried basil can be substituted)
2 cups quick biscuit mix
1 Tbsp. fresh parsley, chopped (optional)

In a saucepan saute onions in margarine (or butter); stir in flour, salt and pepper. Whisk in 2-3/4 cups milk. Cook until slightly thickened. Add next four ingredients. Pour into medium cooking pan. Preheat oven to 450°F. In a medium bowl, combine remaining 3/4 cup milk, the biscuit mix, and (optional) parsley. Drop teaspoonfuls (about 16) of biscuit mixture into the cooking pan mixture. Bake about 15 minutes or until biscuits are browned. Serves 4 - 6.

MARVIN B. HALL

Hawaii Medical Service Association 818 Keeaumoku Street • P.O. Box 860 Honolulu, Hawaii 96808-0860 (808) 944-2110 FAX (808) 944-9419 Branch offices located on Hawaii, Kauai and Maui

KAPIOLANI MEDICAL CENTER
at Pali Momi

When I need a lift in both energy and spirit...what does the trick are the crunchy "ono" cookies made at Kapiolani Medical Center at Pali Momi. Chief Dietician Terri Jones, Chef Nolan Neves and staff, however, are sworn to allow me to have just one... no matter how much I beg!

CRUNCHY "ONO" COOKIES

Yield: 2 Dozen

1 cup	Granulated Sugar
1/2 cup	Margarine
2-1/4 cups	All Purpose Flour
1 teaspoon	Baking Powder
1 whole	Egg
1 teaspoon	Vanilla Extract
3 box (individual size)	Product 19 Cereal
4 oz.	Chopped Walnuts

Cream margarine, sugar and vanilla. Add egg, beat well. Add flour and baking powder. When batter is completely combined, add cereal and walnuts. Bake at 350°F for 20 minutes or until golden brown. Let cool 10 minutes.

Fran Hallonquist

FRANCES A. HALLONQUIST
Chief Executive Officer

98-1079 Moanalua Road • Aiea, Hawaii 96701 • Telephone (808) 486-6000 • FAX (808) 488-1457

OFFICE OF THE MAYOR
CITY AND COUNTY OF HONOLULU
HONOLULU, HAWAII 96813 • AREA CODE 808 • 523-4141

JEREMY HARRIS
MAYOR

HARRIS' QUICK STRAWBERRY PIE RECIPE

3	pints	Fresh Strawberries (larger the better)
1	each	Ready-to-Eat Pie Shell (ready made or recipe of your choice)
1	3.4 oz box	Vanilla Jell-O Instant Pudding & Pie Filling
1	1.2 oz. package	Produce Partners Strawberry Glaze

With the exception of reducing the amount of milk to only 1 1/2 cups, prepare pudding as per directions on box.

Pour into pie shell and refrigerate for at least 30 minutes.

In the meantime...

Prepare strawberry glaze according to directions on the back of the package. (Remember to add boiling water gradually or mixture will not thicken.)

Once glaze is ready, add strawberries and coat thoroughly.

Pour into pie shell on top of pudding.

Refrigerate for approximately one hour so that pie is nicely chilled.

JEREMY HARRIS
Mayor
City & County of Honolulu

RAMONA HARRIS
First Lady
City & County of Honolulu

GTE Hawaiian Tel
GTE Hawaiian Telephone Company Incorporated
P.O. Box 2200 • Honolulu, HI 96841 • 808/546-2323

Beyond the call

Warren H. Haruki
President

Here's an old family favorite recipe that's quick and easy, and guaranteed to *"Broke da Mouth"!*

"Broke da Mouth" Cornbread

3 cups pancake mix
1 cup sugar
2 blocks margarine, melted
3 eggs
1 1/4 cup milk
2 1/2 tsp. baking powder
1/4 cup cornmeal

Combine pancake mix, sugar, baking powder and cornmeal. Beat eggs and milk together with a fork or wire whisk. Add wet ingredients to dry ingredients and mix well. Pour into a greased 9 by 13-inch baking pan. Bake at 350 degrees for 30 minutes.

Warren H. Haruki
President - GTE Hawaiian Tel

Capital Investment of Hawaii, Inc.
Suite 1700 • PRI Tower
733 Bishop Street
PO Box 2668 • Honolulu, Hawaii 96803
Phone: (808) 537-3981 • FAX: (808) 523-3025

Canlis' Special Salad

One way to test a person's age in Hawaii is to ask if he can remember Canlis' Restaurant on Kalakaua Avenue, near the Kuhio Theatre. For the information of the young and recently-arrived, Canlis' was (perhaps still is) the all-time best restaurant in Waikiki. In the days before cholesterol became part of our vocabulary, a great evening started with a Canlis' Special Salad followed by a perfectly grilled steak, a huge baked potato and a Burgandy from Pete's endless bins of *Clos Vougeot Chateau Latour*. All this was served by kimono-clad ladies who made you remember that waiting tables was still a high calling in many parts of the world.

The secret of Pete's salad was that he used lemon juice in his dressing rather than vinegar. That enabled you to discern other flavors in the salad instead of just the overpuckering power of the vinegar, the basic flavoring used by most restaurants today. Before Pete's kids sold the restaurant, I committed his recipe to memory. This ought to be enough for four:

Dressing
Half cup of good olive oil.
1 egg yolk.
Juice of 1 lemon.
Greens
Romaine lettuce, cut at 1 inch intervals.
Chopped mint.
Medium tomatoes, skinned and quartered.
Condiments
4 slices of grilled bacon, chopped
Croutons (best if home made).
Romano cheese, finely grated.

Lightly salt the bowl and rub with a clove of garlic. Add the greens. Mix the dressing and pour over the greens. Mix. Add the condiments. Lightly mix. Serve.

Stuart Ho

FRED H. HONDA
EXECUTIVE MANAGER

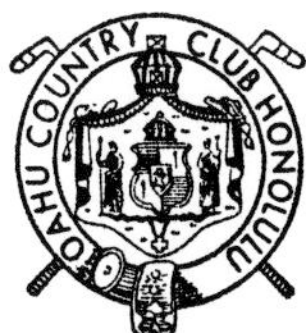

ESTABLISHED 1906
OAHU COUNTRY CLUB
150 COUNTRY CLUB ROAD • HONOLULU, HAWAII 96817
TELEPHONE (808) 595-6331 • FAX (808) 595-3186

SPINACH AND ARTICHOKE CASSEROLE

1 tall can artichoke hearts, or use 3 fresh artichoke hearts, sliced into 6 pieces

2 packages frozen spinach, finely chopped, or use 4 bunches of fresh spinach stemmed, steamed and finely chopped

1 cup medium white sauce made with 2 Tbsp butter, 3 Tbsp flour and 1 cup milk

1/3 cup freshly grated Parmesan cheese

1 cup bread crumbs

Place artichoke hearts in a 1 quart pyrex buttered casserole. Spread the spinach that has been carefully squeezed to eliminate any moisture, over the artichokes. Top with the white sauce, cheese and bread crumbs. Dot with butter and place in a 350° oven for twenty minutes or until lightly brown and bubbly.

Serves six, but easy to double for twelve.

A vegetarian delight which everyone enjoys, yet simple and quick to prepare. Although it may take time to wash, stem and steam the fresh spinach, the entire process may be done the day before and baked just prior to dinner. Your family and guests will be pleased with this dish.

Fred Honda

You will amaze even the most jaded palate with this delicious Caviar Dip. Simple, easy, and quick to prepare in just minutes, it lends an elegant look to your table.

The cost? Very reasonable!
The taste? Very expensive!
Bon Apetite.

CAVIAR DIP

16 oz. cream cheese, softened
1 small onion (finely chopped)
½ cup mayonnaise
½ tsp. cayenne pepper
2 tsp. lemon juice (1 lemon)
2 large (3½ oz. jars) Romanoff black caviar
Carr's Table Water Crackers

Combine first five ingredients. Mold into dome-shaped mound on serving platter. Chill 20-30 minutes until firm. Smooth black caviar onto cream cheese mound to cover completely. (Excess liquid from caviar may be soaked up with a paper towel.) Serve with crackers.

Garnish: Use overlapping lemon wedges around the mound.

Optional: Use low fat cream cheese and mayonnaise.

Mamo Howell

MAMO HOWELL

1020 Auahi Street, Bldg. 6 Honolulu, Hawaii 96814 (808) 592-0611 Fax (808) 592-0621

BENJAMIN J. CAYETANO
GOVERNOR OF HAWAII

LAWRENCE MIIKE
DIRECTOR OF HEALTH

STATE OF HAWAII
DEPARTMENT OF HEALTH
P.O. BOX 3378
HONOLULU, HAWAII 96801

In reply, please refer to:
File: HPED / Nutr

I am honored to be a participant in REHAB's first VIP cookbook. It is a pleasure to support the fine work that REHAB provides to the people of Hawai`i and the Pacific with physical disabilities. Enjoy this easy and tasty salad, It's a favorite in my family.

Chinese Salad

1 large - head lettuce
1 bunch fresh celery
2 large carrots
1 large bell pepper
1 block tofu (firm)
3/4 cup chopped roasted peanuts (unsalted)
1 bunch fresh Chinese parsley

Finely shred lettuce and celery --enough to fill a 9" X 13" serving dish, approximately 2/3 full. Top with shredded carrots and bell pepper. Drain tofu of excess liquid then cut into cubes and place on the vegetable base. Sprinkle chopped roasted peanuts over the tofu and top with chopped Chinese parsley. Chill until ready to serve. Pour Chinese Salad Dressing (recipe below) over the salad just before serving.

Chinese Salad Dressing

2 Tbsp. sugar
1 tsp. salt
1/2 tsp. pepper
1 Tbsp. shoyu
1/4 cup of salad oil
1 Tbsp. sesame oil
3 Tbsp. vinegar
1 Tbsp. sesame seeds (roasted)

Place all ingredients into a container and shake well before using.
Pour over salad just before serving.

Enjoy!

Claire K. Hughes
Chief, Nutrition Branch
RHP Board Member

Hula Girl by David Ka`aihue Oil, 1995

"Painting has helped me regain self esteem, confidence and the spirit to do better."

—David is a mouth stick painter.

Richard L. Humphreys
Chairman & CEO
Bank of America, Hawaii

MUSHROOM CHICKEN SKILLET

2 lb.	boneless, skinless chicken breasts
1	medium clove garlic minced
4 tbsp	butter
1 tbsp	curry powder
2 cups	small mushrooms quartered
1	package dry onion soup mix
3 tbsp	flour
1/2 cup	sliced celery
2 cups	water
1 lb.	fresh asparagus cut into one-inch pieces

Melt butter in large skillet and add garlic and curry powder. Add chicken and saute until golden brown. Add mushrooms and saute 3 - 4 minutes. Stir in soup mix and flour. Gradually add water, stirring constantly. Add celery and cover. Simmer for 20 minutes, stirring occasionally. Add asparagus and cook an additional 10 minutes or until chicken is tender. Serve over rice or noodles. Serves 4.

RICHARD L. HUMPHREYS

Bank of America, FSB
1099 Alakea Street 25th Floor Honolulu, Hawaii 96813 Box 539 Honolulu, Hawaii 96809-0539 808/545-6459

For special company, or casual family dining, this easy-to-prepare main dish can be prepared ahead and set aside for last minute final touches. The flavor, presentation and sophistication of the Mauna Loa Macadamia Nut Sauce will earn you the title of "gourmet chef", and only you will know how easy it was to prepare. Bon Appetite!

Mahimahi with Mauna Loa Macadamia Nut Sauce

For the sauce:

- 2 tablespoons chopped shallot
- 1 tablespoon Mauna Loa Macadamia Nut Oil
- 3 tablespoons dry white wine
- 3/4 cup whipping cream
- Salt to taste
- ½ cup (about 2¼ ounces) Mauna Loa Diced Macadamia Nuts

For the fish:

- 1½ pounds Mahimahi filets (Fresh)
- ¼ cup dry white wine
- 2 tablespoons water
- Salt and freshly ground black pepper to taste

To finish the recipe:

- ½ teaspoon fresh lemon juice
- Salt and freshly ground black pepper to taste
- 4 teaspoons minced fresh parsley
- ¼ cup (about 1 ounce) Mauna Loa Diced Macadamia Nuts

To prepare sauce, place shallot and Macadamia Nut Oil in medium saucepan and saute over low heat, stirring occasionally until soft. Add wine and simmer over moderate heat until mixture is reduced to about 3 tablespoons. Stir in cream and salt and bring to boil, stirring. Cook over moderate heat, stirring often, until mixture is thick enough to coat spoon, 3 to 4 minutes. Cool to lukewarm.

Grind nuts to smooth paste in food processor. With blades turning, gradually pour in cream mixture and process until smooth. Set aside.

To prepare fish, run fingers over filets and carefully pull out any bones with aid of tweezers or sharp paring knife. Arrange fish in one layer in well oiled 10-cup gratin dish or other heavy shallow baking dish. Pour wine and water over fish. Sprinkle lightly with salt and pepper. Set piece of mac nut oiled parchment paper directly on fish to cover it. Bake at 425 degrees about 10 minutes, or until thin skewer inserted into thickest part of filets for about 5 seconds feels hot when touched to underside of wrist.

Carefully remove filets to platter with 2 wide slotted spatulas, reserving cooking liquid. Cover fish with parchment paper to keep it warm. Gradually whisk 2 tablespoons cooking liquid into reserved sauce. Add lemon juice. Season to taste with salt and pepper.

Pat filets dry and spoon sauce over them. Sprinkle with parsley and chopped macadamia nuts. Makes four servings.

Terris H. Inglett

TERRIS H. INGLETT
PRESIDENT

HAWAII AND PACIFIC MARKETING AND SALES
285 SAND ISLAND ACCESS ROAD · SUITE 205 · HONOLULU, HAWAII 96819 · PHONE (808)832-4600 · FAX (808)845-5811

DANIEL K. INOUYE
HAWAII

APPROPRIATIONS
Subcommittee on Defense

COMMERCE, SCIENCE AND TRANSPORTATION

Subcommittee on Surface Transportation
and Merchant Marine

COMMITTEE ON INDIAN AFFAIRS

DEMOCRATIC STEERING COMMITTEE

COMMITTEE ON RULES AND ADMINISTRATION

JOINT COMMITTEE ON PRINTING

United States Senate

SUITE 722, HART SENATE OFFICE BUILDING
WASHINGTON, DC 20510–1102
(202) 224–3934
FAX (202) 224–6747

PRINCE KUHIO FEDERAL BUILDING
ROOM 7325, 300 ALA MOANA BOULEVARD
HONOLULU, HI 96850–4975
(808) 541–2542
FAX (808) 541–2549

101 AUPUNI STREET, NO. 205
HILO, HI 96720
(808) 935–0844
FAX (808) 961–5163

MAGGIE INOUYE'S PAPAYA CHEESE PIE

2 Hawaiian papayas, peeled, halved and seeded
1 tbsp. cornstarch
1 lb. cream cheese, softened
1/3 cup sugar
3 eggs
1 tsp. grated lemon peel
1 9-inch baked pastry crust
Kiwi slices
Mint sprigs

Puree one papaya in blender to make 1/2 cup (turn motor on and off and scrape sides of container as needed). Combine puree with cornstarch; set aside. In mixing bowl, beat cream cheese with sugar to blend well. Mix in eggs and lemon peel, then stir in reserved papaya puree. Pour into crust.

Bake in 375 degree oven 25 to 30 minutes until just set. Cool. Top with remaining papaya, thinly sliced. Brush with melted jelly to glaze. Garnish with kiwi slices and mint.

Makes 6 to 8 servings.

Dan

DANIEL K. INOUYE
United States Senator

A Jardine Pacific business

Theo H. Davies & Co., Ltd.
841 Bishop Street, Suite 2300
Honolulu, Hawaii 96813-3923

808/532-6500

Word of the request for one of *my* recipes infiltrated the office. Work stopped; followed by a solid 35 minutes of uncontrollable laughter. When it comes to culinary talents -- I don't get no respect. Naturally, I docked everybody 45 minutes -- the extra 10 minutes was for punitive damages, for mental anguish, pain, suffering, etc.

My wife, Terry, laughed louder and longer and docked me 45 minutes. Being a very perceptive person, I got the message and submit my wife's recipe for a quick, easy and I might add very tasty dish.

ITALIAN LOW CALORIE POTATO SALAD

Red potatoes, whole, washed and unpeeled
Paul Newman's Light Italian Dressing

Place the potatoes in a pot of boiling water. Bring the water to a second boil. Cover the pot and reduce the heat. Cook the potatoes until tender but still firm -- about 10 to 15 minutes. Drain the potatoes and dice into 1/2 to 3/4 inch pieces. Add the Italian dressing and mix thoroughly. Cover the salad and refrigerate until ready to serve.

Martin J. Jaskot
President and Chief Executive Officer

Fax: 808/532-6544

MAUI
INTER•CONTINENTAL
RESORT

3700 Wailea Alanui
Kihei · Wailea · Maui · Hawaii 96753
808 · 879 · 1922

This is a wonderful dish I discovered after fishing for salmon in Alaska. Upon my return to the islands, I created this flavorful Hawaiian dish. This dish is quick and easy to prepare and I'm sure you'll agree the result is quite spectacular!

Grilled Alaskan Salmon with Fresh Hawaiian Lychee Salsa and Macadamia Nut & Lime Vinaigrette

(serves one)

For Fish:

- 8 oz. salmon
- Salt & pepper to taste
- 1/4 oz. olive oil

*Grill salmon on barbecue or saute indoors

For Salsa:

- 4 lychees (peeled, seeded, and diced)
- 1/2 oz. green onion—fine cut
- 5 leafs of coriander
- 1 oz. Maui onion
- 2 tablespoons of olive oil
- 1 tomato (peeled, seeded, and diced)
- 1 each lime juice
- 1 each Hawaiian chili pepper (chop fine, no seeds)
- Salt & pepper to taste
- 1 tablespoon of Maui honey

*Mix all ingredients in bowl except salt, pepper and olive oil. Mix well; then add seasoning and finish with olive oil. Place salsa on plate and put the cooked salmon on top.

For Vinaigrette:

- 1 tablespoon of fresh lime juice
- Salt & pepper to taste
- 1/2 oz. Macadamia Nuts chopped fine
- 1 oz. olive oil

*Mix all ingredients and pour over fish.

I hope you enjoy!

Warm Aloha!

Brad Jencks
General Manager

LAWRENCE M. JOHNSON
Chairman of the Board
Chief Executive Officer

BANKOH CHOCOLATE CHIP COOKIES

1 cup butter

2 cups white sugar

2 eggs

1 teaspoon vanilla

3 cups flour

1/2 tablespoon salt

1 tablespoon soda

1 package chocolate chips

1 1/2 cups macadamia nuts

Cream butter and sugar. Add eggs, vanilla and then chocolate chips. Mix in 2 cups flour and add mixture of 1 cup flour, salt, and soda. Stir in mac nuts. Bake at 350 degrees for 10-15 minutes.

POST OFFICE BOX 2900 • HONOLULU, HAWAII 96846 • TELEPHONE (808) 537-8111 • FAX (808) 521-7602

Mike Kallay, *President and Publisher*

It is my honor to be invited to submit a recipe for the First Edition of the VIP Cookbook, sponsored by the wonderful people of Rehabilitation Hospital of the Pacific Foundation. Mahalo.

As a native and lifelong resident of Louisville — and as one of the newest of newcomers to this remarkable community and state — I thought it might be "fun" to offer a recipe indigenous to Kentucky because bourbon whiskey is a major beverage of choice by adults here.

Kentucky Mint Julep

Ingredients: Kentucky bourbon whiskey. (Recommended brands, in order: Maker's Mark, Old Forester, Early Times and Jim Beam. Not recommended: Jack Daniel's, Canadian Club, Crown Royal, etc., because they're **NOT** bourbon.) Fresh mint. Granulated sugar. Powdered sugar. Shaved ice. Water.

Glasses you should use (9 oz.): Silver "julep cups," aluminum cups or glass glasses, in that order. Chill in a freezer for a least an hour prior to use. (Never use paper, plastic, etc.).

The "concoction":

1. Mint extract. Pluck 30 mint leaves per 3/4 liter of bourbon. Soak in bowl with 3-4 oz. of bourbon for 15 minutes. Remove leaves and place on a cotton cloth. Wring the cloth containing leaves tightly over bowl. Immerse cloth-wrapped mint in bowl and wring dry.

2. Syrup. Heat equal parts of granulated sugar and water. Stir until well-blended (liquid turns clear).

3. Blend seven parts bourbon with two parts syrup. Add mint extract to taste.

Fill chilled cup/glass with shaved ice. Add 5 oz. of mint julep and garnish mint sprigs and a sprinkling of powdered sugar on top.

This Mint Julep is a conglomeration of several people's, including my Mother, Bill Samuels Jr., CEO of Maker's Mark (he distills the finest bourbon in the world), and me.

But perhaps the legendary Henry Watterson — longtime editor of the Louisville Courier-Journal and a titan of 20th century journalism — had **THE** best julep recipe.

After preparing all the ingredients, "Marse" Henry once said, "Throw 'em out and drink the bourbon straight!"

IOLANI SPORTSWEAR, LTD.

1234 Kona Street, Honolulu Hawaii • Telephone (808) 597-1044 • FAX (808) 591-8529

The young, the old, all will enjoy these Tofu Patties. They are good for your health too! We use a little bit of this, a little bit of that--whatever is available. Eliminate or add ingredients according to your taste and fancy.

TOFU PATTIES

1 block tofu (water squeezed out)
1 small can water chestnuts, chopped
8 ounces imitation crab meat, chopped
4 ounces uncooked fishcake mix
1 tsp. parsley, minced
1 Tbsp. minced green onion, round onion or chives
1/2 kamaboko, chopped, for color and flavor (optional)
Egg whites from 2 eggs
Grated carrots
Salt and pepper to taste

Mix all ingredients and form into patties. Fry until golden brown in oiled pan (oil makes them crispy on the outside and adds flavor). For more flavor, try mixing Mazola oil with sesame oil when frying.

Enjoy!

KEIJI KAWAKAMI
President

OUTRIGGER
ENTERPRISES™

Richard R. Kelley
Chairman of the Board

Here's a recipe for a five bean salad that is a great addition to buffets and barbecues. Because it has always been my personal favorite, the kids and grandkids call it:

PAPA'S BEAN SALAD

1-15 oz. can	Green Beans
1-15 oz. can	Yellow Beans
1-15 oz. can	Red Kidney Beans
1-15 oz. can	Bean Sprouts
1-15 oz. can	Garbanzo Beans
1 whole	Onion, chopped
1-2 oz. can	Mushrooms
1-6 oz. jar	Marinated Artichoke Hearts, chopped

Liquid

3/4 cup	Sugar
1 tsp.	Salt
1 tsp.	Pepper
1/3 cup	Salad Oil (not olive oil)
2/3 cup	Wine Vinegar

•Mix all ingredients in a bowl
•Cover and put in refrigerator overnight
•Serve chilled

Richard R. Kelley

Hotel Operating Co. of Hawaii, Ltd. • Outrigger Hotels Hawaii • Outrigger Marketing, Inc. • Outrigger Hotels USA, Inc.

2375 Kuhio Avenue • Honolulu, Hawaii 96815-2939
Telephone: 808-921-6610 • Facsimile: 808-921-6655

ALBERT C.
KOBAYASHI, INC.
GENERAL CONTRACTORS
Gentry Business Park • 94-535 Uke'e Street
Waipahu, Hawaii 96797 • Phone (808) 671-6460 • FAX 676-5832

BUTTER POUND CAKE

1 box Duncan Hines Butter Cake Mix
1 carton sour cream (8 oz.)
1 block butter (melted)
1/4 cup sugar
1/4 cup Wesson oil
1 tsp. vanilla
4 eggs

Mix cake mix and sugar first, add sour cream, butter, oil, vanilla, then eggs. Beat for 2 minutes with an electric beater. Pour into 2 greased and floured loaf pans. Bake at 350 degrees for 45 minutes.

Top with fresh strawberries, ice cream or just have it plain.

Bert A. Kobayashi
Chairman/CEO

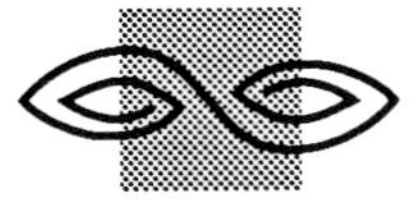

Robert Lee Jr MD
Ophthalmology

Pauahi Tower Suite 310
1001 Bishop Street
Honolulu Hawaii 96813
Telephone 808 536 0400

Pearlridge Shopping Center
Phase II Mall Level
Aiea Hawaii 96701
Telephone 808 486 8939

508 Atkinson Drive
Honolulu Hawaii 96814
Telephone 808 949 7288

I enjoy experimenting in the kitchen when we entertain guests. I often prepare Fish Tartare served as an Hors d'oeuvre or as a first course. You can always improvise or add to the tartare as by using besides the white fish, pink-reddish ahi or a fillet of fresh salmon or make three types. It seems to be a palate pleaser as it combines a touch of the islands with a bit of the french and besides, it is appealing to the eye.

FISH TARTARE

1 1/2 lbs of fresh white fish, such as Swordfish, Ulua, Au or may use Ahi, coarsely chopped
1 small Maui onion, chopped fine
3 tsp dijon mustard
2 Tbsp capers, squeeze out brine and chop
2 tsp dill
1 tsp anchovy paste
2 Tbsp chopped parsley
5 Tbsp mayonnaise
2 tsp brandy
Salt, black and white pepper to taste
cucumbers
crackers

As a First Course

Tartare as above
Shiso leaf (perilla) or red lettuce
(Shiso available at Taniguchi Store)
3 rose potatoes, 2 yams, 2 purple Japanese sweet potatoes (boil, peel and sliced)
Tobiko, Kaneko, Ebiko, salmon roe, or caviar
2 or 3 stems of chives
olive oil
Baguette french bread

To the chopped Maui onion, add a pinch of Hawaiian salt, mix and squeeze out the juice. Mix all ingredients and chill. Serve with crackers and cucumbers sliced on a diagonal. Serves 8 - 10 people but too much is not enough.

As a first course, place 2 Tbsp tartare on one or two shiso leaves or red lettuce leaf. Shiso has a mint fruit flavor. Top tartare with 1/2 tsp of Tobiko, Kaneko or Ebiko (flying fish, crab or shrimp roe obtained at Shirokiya's or Tamashiro's Market.) May use salmon roe or caviar or all separately on the plate. Arrange a few slices of the potatoes sprinkle on a dash of olive oil and chopped chives. It is a palette of color. Goes well with a sauvignon blanc wine. Seconds anyone?

Robert Lee Jr., MD
Bailli, Honolulu Chapter
Chaine des Rotisseurs

This is a favorite of the Leong clan. It is so easy to prepare and is enjoyed after a filling meal or during the warm months. Quite refreshing!

Almond Custard

2 Tbsp. plain gelatin	3/4 cup sugar (more if desired)
3 cups water*	3 tsp. Almond extract
3 1/2 cups milk* (your choice)	Fruits (optional)

Soften gelatin in 1/2 cup water. Combine water and sugar; bring to a boil. Add softened gelatin and cook for 2 minutes or until gelatin dissolves. Remove from heat - add milk and almond extract. Pour into custard cups or individual bowls. Chill. Serve with mixed fruit; lychee; loongan (dragon eye); or fresh cubed melon(s) if desired.

Makes approximately 12 servings.

* If you wish a firmer custard, reduce the liquids to:
1 1/2 cups water; and 2 cups milk. Pour into a 9" X 13" pan. Chill until firm. Cut into squares and serve in bowl topped with fruits. Makes approximately 8 servings.

Enjoy!

Edith Leong
REHAB Foundation

226 North Kuakini Street • Honolulu, Hawaii 96817 • Telephone: (808) 544-3302 • FAX: (808) 544-3335

REHABILITATION HOSPITAL OF THE PACIFIC

Anyone lucky enough to spend some time working for the REHAB family as a volunteer cannot help but be impressed by the little miracles which occur everyday, as these dedicated people help others rebuild their lives. They even have time-saving tips for old favorites like Chinese gau, that help to make volunteering a snap.

MICROWAVE GAU
(Chinese New Year Pudding)

1 pound Chinese brown brick sugar
2 1/2 cups hot water
3 cups (1 pound) mochiko, sifted
1/4 cup salad oil
2 teaspoons toasted sesame seeds
1 dried red date

Dissolve the brown brick sugar in hot water and let cool.
Gradually add the mochiko, stirring to make a thin batter.
Stir in salad oil.
Pour batter into a 2-quart greased, microwave-safe bowl, covering loosely with plastic wrap.
Cook in microwave 15 to 18 minutes on high, turning bowl 1/4 way around twice during cooking.
Garnish center with red date and sprinkle top with sesame seeds.

Jan Luke Loo

Janice Luke Loo
Vice Chair, REHAB Foundation
Capital Campaign Chair

REHABILITATION HOSPITAL OF THE PACIFIC FOUNDATION
CAPITAL CAMPAIGN

226 North Kuakini Street • Honolulu, Hawaii, USA 96817 • Phone (808) 544-3302 • Facsimile (808) 544-3335

WARREN K.K. LUKE
Vice Chairman and CEO

Here's a recipe that's so versatile, it can be served for breakfast, as an accompaniment for lunch or dinner, as a dessert to top off a meal, or as a snack any time of day. Another great feature of this recipe is its simplicity -- it's easy enough for anyone to prepare -- even me! It's also a good way to get rid of old bananas.

BANANA BREAD

Mix and sift:	1-1/4 cup flour 1/2 tsp. salt 1 tsp. baking soda 1 cup sugar
Add:	1 block butter, softened [1/4 lb.] -- (Use hand) 2 eggs, well-beaten 4 ripened bananas, mashed well (Add bananas with fork, folding into other ingredients)

Pour batter into greased and floured baking dish or loaf pan and bake at 350 degrees for 30 to 40 minutes.

WARREN K. K. LUKE

45 North King Street, Honolulu, Hawaii • Telephone (808) 528-7711 Mailing Address: P. O. Box 3740, Honolulu, Hawaii 96812

I am personally aware of the tremendous job that Rehabilitation Hospital Of The Pacific has done for the people of our community. A few years ago, you helped my mother recover from major surgery to her back which had affected her ability to walk. She turned a healthy 80 last fall! Thanks for all your kokua. I'm honored that you would consider me to participate in this worthwhile project.

Many years ago, the Club was looking for a signature Iced Tea. I had been to a number of restaurants and clubs, tasting their specialty iced teas without success in finding something that was simple to make that had great taste too. Finally, a member, Mrs. Dorothy Ito told me to try an iced tea that she had made at home. I tried the tea and it was delightful with just the right balance of sweet versus tart. Voila, Plantation Iced Tea was born. It is the perfect thirst quencher after 18 holes of golf or three sets of tennis and embarrassingly easy to make.

WAIALAE COUNTRY CLUB
PLANTATION ICED TEA

1 tub	Crystal Light Iced Tea (Natural Flavor)
3 ozs.	Dole 100% Unsweetened Pineapple Juice
54 ozs.	Water

Dissolve the Crystal Light Iced Tea in 54 ozs. of water. The instructions on the tub indicate that you should use 64 ozs. but we have found that 54 ozs. works better. Add 3 ozs. of the Unsweetened Pineapple Juice and mix thoroughly. Pour into iced glass. Use pineapple slice and/or mint leaf for garnish (optional).

Note: The tea is also low in calories. An 8 oz. serving is approximately 10 calories.

Allan S.U. Lum, CCM
General Manager

4997 KAHALA AVENUE • HONOLULU, HAWAII 96816 • TELEPHONE (808) 734-2151 • FAX (808) 734-4791

WORLD WIDE TOURS & TRAVEL SERVICE INC
1120 Nuuanu Avenue
Honolulu, Hawaii 96817
Phone: (808) 533-3691
Fax: (808) 536-1000

BEANCURD WITH PORK HASH AND CHILI SAUCE

This Oriental favorite dish is very nutritious, tasty and easy to make.

INGREDIENTS:

2lbs. Beancurd, diced to 3/4 inch cubes

½lb. Ground Pork

2 Chili Pepper, chopped or chili sauce

½ cup Onion, chopped (optional)

½ Tbsp Garlic, grated

4 Tbsp Oyster Sauce or Soy Sauce

½ tsp Cornstarch, mix to a paste with water

4 Tbsp Cooking Oil

METHOD:

Heat oil in skillet. Saute onion and garlic. Add pork and stir cook for about 4 minutes. Add beancurd, pepper, oyster sauce and sugar. Bring to a boil. Thicken with cornstarch paste. Mix well. Serve hot. **ENJOY!!!**

WORLDWIDE TOURS & TRAVEL SERVICE

Betsy Au Lum

BETSY AU LUM, PRESIDENT

2305 KAMEHAMEHA HWY. • P.O. BOX 30707
HONOLULU, HAWAII 96820
RETAIL/WILL CALL 842-2225
WELDING 842-2222
SAFETY 824-2222
GASES 842-2222
MEDICAL EQUIPMENT 842-2218
FAX 842-2136

BRANCHES:
HILO 935-3341
KONA 329-7393
KAMUELA 885-8636
KAHULUI 877-0056
LIHUE 245-6766
WAIPAHU 671-5435

GASPRO BAR-B-QUE BABY BACK RIBS

Here is a recipe that makes that weekend Bar-B-Que not only "finger licking good" but simple with a little bit of advance preparation. Make sure to prepare extra portions as people will return for seconds and even third helpings. Also be sure to have lots of napkins on hand.

One Day Ahead of Time

Prepare Ribs :

- Using three (3) to four (4) complete slabs of baby back ribs, cut them into sections of two (2) to three (3) ribs per section.
- Place in a large pot of boiling water.
- Add:

1	quartered onion
1	bay leaf
1	clove garlic - crushed
2	teaspoons salt

- Boil ribs for one (1) hour or until meat begins to separate from the bones.

Sauce:

2	cloves garlic - crushed
1	cup shoyu (soy sauce)
1/2	cup catsup
2	or more teaspoons chili powder - to taste
9 oz.	Honey
1/4	teaspoon ginger

Marinate Ribs

- Remove ribs from pot and coat on both sides with sauce
- Marinate over night

The Big Day

- Bar-B-Que ribs over medium to high fire
- Baste ribs with extra sauce
- Only Bar-B-Que ribs long enough to heat them up as they were pre-cooked the previous day.

Edward MacNaughton
President

Simply Delicious Artichoke & Cheese Dip

To shatter one of the myths in my office about my cooking abilities, I want to share one of my favorite recipes. It isn't called "Simply Delicious" for nothing. First of all, it is delicious, and more importantly, it's simple to make...so simple that even I can make it! And... this dip goes well with all my catered meals!

Ingredients

- 2 cups Monterey Jack cheese, shredded
- 1/2 cup Parmesan, shredded
- 2 small jars marinated artichoke hearts, drained and chopped
- 1/2 cup mayonnaise
- 1 cup cheddar cheese, shredded
- 1/4 cup salsa
- Tabasco sauce to taste - I like it *hot*...about 1/2 tsp.

Topping

- 1/4 cup cheddar cheese, shredded
- 2 Tbsp. salsa

Pre-heat oven to 350 degrees. In a large bowl combine all ingredients except topping ingredients; mix well. Transfer to a quiche or pie plate.

Topping: Place cheddar cheese on top in a circle approx. 4" in diameter. Pour the salsa inside the circle. Bake for 20 minutes, or until bubbly. Transfer pie plate on a platter and surround with tortilla chips.

Simple to make, attractive to serve, and delicious to eat...Ole'!

E. Lynne Madden
Executive Vice President

99-880 IWAENA STREET
HONOLULU, HAWAII · 96701-3202
TEL 808 · 487 · 7299 · FAX 808 · 488 · 2279

hopaco

Boise Cascade
Office Products
Distribution Division

2833 Paa Street
Honolulu, Hawaii 96819-4406
808/831-8611
Fax: 808/831-8690
808/831-8698

Donna and I took a sabbatical during 1989 through 1991 and sailed throughout the Caribbean on our sailboat. This "boat" recipe is a quick, easy, low-fat meal that complemented many a sunset.

Spinach and Clam Linguini

1 14 oz can of diced tomatoes
1 6.5 oz can of chopped or minced clams
1 small can of chopped spinach
- garlic salt to taste
1/4 cup Kraft grated parmesan cheese
- Linguini for 4 servings

While pasta is cooking, simmer together all other ingredients except the cheese.

Drain the cooked pasta and serve topped with the sauce and cheese.

Great served with garlic toast!

Bill
Bill Matheson
General Manager

Two Worlds by John Elmore — Mixed media, 1994

"John was the inspiration for the concept of REHAB's creative arts program. The program was an opportunity for John to express himself artistically and emotionally in the last year of his life."

—by Tara Sullivan, Recreational Therapist

M. Matoi
Hair Studio · Honolulu

VIETNAMESE SPRING ROLL

2 LBS. GROUND PORK OR GROUND CHICKEN
2 LBS. RAW SHRIMP (SHELLED AND COARSELY CHOPPED)
10 FRESH WHOLE PIECES OF BLACK FUNGUS THINLY CUT. OR 1-1/2 CUPS OF ALREADY CUT DRIED BLACK FUNGUS. SOAK DRIED BLACK FUNGUS IN WATER TILL SOFT. CHANGE WATER TWICE TO CLEAN OUT DIRT.
4 OZ. DRIED LONG RICE SHORTLY CUT.
1 SMALL ONION FINELY CHOPPED
1 SMALL CAN WATER CHESTNUTS FINELY CHOPPED
2 TSP. FINELY GRATED GARLIC OR ABOUT 4 PIECES OF GRATED GARLIC.
5 STEMS OF GREEN ONIONS FINELY CHOPPED

ADD AND MIX TOGETHER:
1 TSP. SALT
2 TSP. FISH SAUCE (PATIS)
6 TSP. SUGAR
1 TSP. PEPPER
2 PACKAGES LUMPIA WRAPPER (30 IN EACH PACKAGE)

WRAP INGREDIENTS IN LUMPIA WRAPPERS. EACH ROLL SHOULD BE LARGER THAN THE SIZE OF A HOT DOG. DEEP FRY EACH ROLL OVER MEDIUM HEAT UNTIL GOLDEN BROWN. THEN PUT ROLLS ON PAPER TOWEL TO ABSORB THE EXCESS OIL. CUT EACH ROLL IN HALF.
WRAP SPRING ROLLS IN BUTTER LETTUCE AND ADD A LITTLE PIECE OF PARSLEY, MINT AND/OR BASIL.

SPRING ROLL SAUCE:
4 TSP. FISH SAUCE
4 TSP. VINEGAR
4 TSP. WATER
4 TSP. CONCENTRATED LEMON JUICE
3 OZ. SUGAR
1 TSP. GARLIC FINELY GRATED
1 TSP. HAWAIIAN CHILI PEPPER FINELY CHOPPED OR MEXICAN CHILI PEPPER
STRAIN SAUCE INGREDIENTS TO TAKE OUT EXCESS GARLIC AND CHILI PEPPER SEED.

Milton Matoi
M. MATOI HAIR STUDIO

The Galerie at Imperial Plaza
725 Kapiolani Blvd., Suite 209
Honolulu, Hawaii 96813
(808) 596-0855

THE PLAZA CLUB
HAWAII

A Plaza Club favorite!

Cream Brulee

2 1/2 cup heavy cream
1/2 cup packed light brown sugar
6 egg yolks
1 vanilla bean split in half lengthwise
4 to 6 Tbsp granulated sugar

Place all ingredients in small saucepan. Place over medium heat until hot but not boiling, stirring constantly. Place 4, 8oz ramakins (souffle cups) on a baking dish - divide hot cream mixture into them. Set 4 ramakins in a baking dish. Place in a 300°F oven. Pour enough hot water in baking dish to come 1/2 way up sides of ramakins. Bake for 1 hour or until custard is set. Remove from oven and refrigerate at least 6 hours.

Evenly spread 1 1/2 Tbsp sugar over top of each custard. Place under hot broiler until sugar carmalizes. Remove and enjoy!

Kay Mattos
Club Manager

Club Quarters: 20th Floor, Pioneer Plaza • 900 Fort Street
Honolulu, Hawaii 96813 • (808) 521-8905 • Fax: (808) 531-4769

Rehabilitation Hospital of the Pacific • 226 North Kuakini Street • Honolulu, HI 96817 • Telephone: (808) 531-3511 • FAX: 544-3335

Curried Chicken and Spinach Salad

(Serves 4)

This is a refreshing change of pace for lunch or a light dinner. Serve with crusty warm bread. If you wish, you may omit the chicken, or substitute cooked turkey (a great way to use the holiday left-overs!).

2 pounds fresh spinach
2 crisp red delicious apples, unpeeled
2/3 cup dry-roasted Spanish peanuts
1/3 cup thinly sliced green onions
2 Tbsp. toasted sesame seeds
1 cup diced cooked chicken or turkey
1/2 cup seedless raisins

Dressing

1/2 cup white vinegar
1/2 - 2/3 cup Canola or other light salad oil
1 Tbsp. finely chopped chutney
1 tsp. curry powder, to taste
1 tsp. salt, to taste
1 tsp. dry mustard
1/4 tsp. Tabasco sauce

Trim, discard tough spinach stems, rinse well and pat dry. Break into bite-size pieces. Wrap in towel, chill.

Core and dice unpeeled apples; add the remaining salad ingredients.

Arrange the apple mixture in a serving bowl over a bed of spinach; top with the chicken or turkey.

Combine the dressing ingredients and mix well. Just before serving, pour over the salad and toss gently.

Sally McDermott
Sally McDermott
Board of Directors
Rehabilitation Hospital of the Pacific, Inc.

Richard E. Meiers
President/CEO

New Years Chicken Salad

2 quarts cooked chicken
2 lbs. seedless grapes
2 cups sliced celery
3 cups mayonnaise
1 tbsp. curry powder
Boston or bib lettuce
1 large can (20 oz.) water chestnuts
2 or 3 cups toasted slivered almonds
2 tbsp. soy sauce
1 large can pineapple chunks (cut in half)

Cut chicken into bite size pieces. Slice water chestnuts. Wash grapes and cut in half. Add sliced celery, pineapple, and 2-2 1/2 cups toasted almonds. Mix above ingredients. Mix the mayonnaise with the curry powder and soy. Combine with the chicken and chill for several hours. (Best if made the day before.) To serve, spoon into lettuce nests. Sprinkle top of salad with additional toasted almonds. Serves 12 generously.

Rick Meiers
RICHARD E. MEIERS
President/CEO

932 Ward Avenue Suite 430 Honolulu, Hawaii 96814-2126 808/521-8961 FAX: 808/599-2879

Affiliated with the American Hospital Association
and the American Health Care Association

People who know me would bet on my golf game before they would bet on my cooking. Since everyone knows that my cooking skills are limited, I wisely borrowed a special recipe from my Mom, who mastered egg rolls and golf as well!

Mother's Egg Rolls

1/2 pound fresh shrimp
1 cup cooked ground pork
1/2 cup green onions
1 tsp. sugar
1/4 tsp. ajinomoto (optional)
1 Tbsp. peanut butter
1 cup chopped celery
1/2 cup chopped water chestnuts
2 tsp. salt
1/8 tsp. pepper
1 Tbsp. melted butter
2 packages egg roll wrappers (Won Ton Pi wrappers also work well.)

Shell shrimp and place in strainer. Pour hot water over shrimp then chop fine. Combine all ingredients in bowl and mix well until thoroughly blended. (If dry, add butter.) Mixture should appear moist. Cool mixture before rolling in egg roll wrappers. Deep fry, drain and serve.

Enjoy!

Ko Miyataki
President

Brandi's Deli
Catering Services Available

We are honored to be invited to participate in the first edition of the VIP cookbook, for such a good cause like the Rehabilitation Hospital of the Pacific. We hope the proceeds from the cookbook will help meet the hospital's goals. Enjoy this recipe of onolicious spare ribs with a little local flavah.

Sweet and Sour Spare Ribs

Sauce:

1 cup shoyu

1 cup vinegar

1 1/2 cup sugar

1 cup pineapple juice

5 lbs. spare ribs

Boil ribs with 3 ginger slices. (30 min.) Rinse. Add sauce, cook until tender. Approx. 30 min. Thicken with corn starch. Served topped with pineapple chunks.

Stanley Nambu

STANLEY NAMBU
President

1600 Kapiolani Boulevard • Suite 122 • Honolulu, Hawaii 96814

President

This is a recipe that has been in my wife's family for three generations. Her Scottish grandmother passed it on to her daughter who then passed it on to my wife and I reap the benefits of this tradition. We hope you enjoy it too!

Grandmother-In-Law's Cornflake Cookies

1/4 lb. butter
1/4 lb. sugar
1/2 cup sultanas (golden raisins)
6 ozs. self rising flour
1 egg

Cream butter and sugar. Add egg, flour and sultanas. Take 1 tsp. of mixture and roll in crushed cornflakes. Drop on cookie sheet, allowing room to spread, and bake in moderate oven (325°) until golden brown.

Henry Neal

HENRY NEAL

BHP Hawaii Inc
733 Bishop Street
PO Box 3379 Honolulu Hawaii 96842 USA
Telephone 808 547 3111 Facsimile 808 547 3145

ERNST & YOUNG LLP

■ 2400 Pauahi Tower
1001 Bishop Street
Honolulu, Hawaii 96813

■ Phone: 808 531 2037

This recipe is simpler than it looks and a great way to enjoy steaks. It also proves that you can cook a delicious steak without grilling (barbecuing) it. Good luck!

FILET MIGNON IN COGNAC CREAM SAUCE

4 filet mignons - cut 1 1/4" thick
Fresh ground pepper
1 tsp. salt
4 Tbsp. unsalted butter
1 Tbsp. vegetable oil
2 shallots, minced
1/2 cup heavy cream
1 tsp. fresh lemon juice
1/2 cup Cognac

1. Season steaks with pepper and marinate in 1/4 cup of Cognac at room temperature, turning occasionally, for 30 minutes. Remove steaks, pat dry, and season with salt. Reserve the marinade.

2. In a heavy skillet, melt 2 Tbsp. butter in the oil, over high heat. Sear the steaks, until well browned (2 minutes per side). Reduce heat to moderate and cook 8 more minutes for medium rare.

3. Remove steaks and keep warm in foil. Pour off fat, melt the balance of the butter, add the shallots, cook till softened (about 1 minute).

4. Pour in marinade and 1/4 cup Cognac. Increase heat to bring to a boil. Scrape the brown bits off skillet, cook until reduced by 1/2. Add cream and boil till reduced by 1/2 again. Season with lemon juice, salt and pepper.

5. Spoon the sauce over the steaks and serve with rice or a simple potato and a green salad.

J. Edd New
Managing Partner

HAWAIIAN'S HAUPIA SQUARES

CRUST:

1-1/2 Blocks Butter, Softened
4 Tbsp. Granulated Sugar
1-1/2 Cups Flour
1/2 Cup Macadamia Nuts, Chopped

Cream butter and sugar; add flour and nuts.
Press into ungreased 13" X 9" pan and bake for 20 minutes at 350°.
Cool.

HAUPIA LAYER:

2 Cans Coconut Milk
1 Cup Granulated Sugar
2-1/2 Cups Water

3/4 Cup Cornstarch
1/2 Cup Water

1 8 Oz. Cool Whip Tub

Mix cornstarch and 1/2 cup water. Set aside.
Mix coconut milk, sugar and water in saucepan. Cook over medium heat until mixture bubbles. Turn the heat off and add cornstarch mixture while stirring continuously for approximately four (4) minutes. Cool, pour over crust and chill four (4) hours or overnight. Top with Cool Whip and grated coconut flakes (opt.).

Bruce R. Nobles
Chairman, President and
Chief Executive Officer

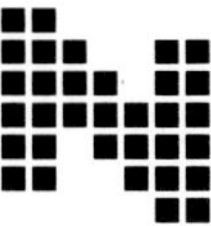

Benjamin S. **Notkin**/Hawaii Ltd

Consulting Mechanical Engineers
210 Ward Avenue • Suite 220
Honolulu • Hawaii 96814
Phone: (808) 523-1363
Fax: (808) 526-3548

Not only is this easy, but it's an unusual combination of tastes and it's an attractive presentation.

Spinach Strawberry Salad

11 oz. fresh spinach, washed, dried well and cut into bite sized pieces
8 oz. fresh strawberries, washed, dried, sliced

Dressing:

1 egg yolk
1 Tbsp. lemon juice
1/4 cup sugar
1/4 - 1/2 cup olive oil

Combine egg yolk, lemon juice and sugar in small bowl. Mix well and add olive oil, very slowly, beating with electric beater or use a food processor. Cover and refrigerate for six to eight hours.

To serve, pour cold dressing over chilled salad.

Benj. S. Notkin

Benjamin S. Notkin

Japan Airlines
Regional Office, Hawaii
1132 Bishop Street, Suite 1500
Honolulu, Hawaii 96813
Fax Number: (808) 544-8285

GYOZA
(Potstickers)

1/2 pound ground pork
1 pound chopped won bok cabbage
1/4 cup chopped green onion
1 1/2 tsp salt
2 tbsp shoyu
1 tbsp sake
1 tbsp shortening oil
1 tbsp sesame oil
1 tbsp grated ginger
1-3 cloves garlic, grated
30 round wonton wrappers

Put all ingredients in mixing bowl and stir well with hand. Divide meat filling into 30 balls and place on center of wonton wrappers. Fold each wrapper in half, brush edge with water, and seal by pleating edges, forming half-moon shape.

Preheat skillet with 1 tbsp oil. Put gyoza in single layer in skillet and brown bottoms. Then pour in 1/2 cup water, cover skillet and cook till steam is gone.
Repeat till all gyoza are cooked.

Serve with shoyu-vinegar sauce; add hot sauce if desired.

Tadamichi Okubo
Vice President & Regional Manager
Hawaii

FINANCE FACTORS, LTD.

A member of the Finance Factors Family

WENDELL K. PANG
Vice Chairman of the Board
Chief Executive Officer

Spicy Louisiana Lima Beans

2 bags of dry lima beans
3 ham hocks
1 package of salt pork (par-boiled to remove some of the salt)
2 bay leaves
5-10 leaves of basil
1 can of solid pack tomatoes (optional)
1 portuguese sausage, sliced
1 round onion, chopped
1 chili pepper or cayenne pepper (optional)

Soak lima beans overnight in cold water. In the meantime, place ham hocks, bay leaves and basil in a crock pot with at least 1-2 quarts water and cook overnight.

The next day, drain the beans and add them to the crock pot with the ham hocks and soup stock. (If the crock pot is too full, simmer this on the stove top for at least two to three hours). When the consistency is like a thick stew, add portuguese sausage, onion, salt pork and tomatoes.

Season to taste by adding salt, pepper, a touch of sugar, and some cayenne pepper. This dish is easy to prepare when you use the crock pot to cook the meal!

Wendell K. Pang

1164 Bishop Street, Suite 800 • Honolulu, Hawaii 96813-2810 • Telephone: (808) 548-3311 • Facsimile: (808) 548-3367

Honolulu Publishing Company, Ltd.

36 MERCHANT STREET HONOLULU, HAWAI'I 96813 (808) 524-7400 FAX (808) 531-2306

Colorful, Crunchy Cole Slaw

This cool, crunchy salad is low in fat, high in taste and a great accompaniment to BBQs, grilled fish, burgers—even sandwiches. Serve in a glass or acrylic bowl for eye appeal. Serves 6-8.

1/2 head green cabbaage, shredded
1/2 head red cabbage, shredded
3 carrots, grated
2 celery stalks, diced
4 green onions, diced
1/2 green pepper, thinly sliced
1 small red Jalapeño pepper, finely sliced
1/4 cup olive oil
1/4 cup balsamic (or your favorite) vinegar
1/4 tsp. garlic salt
1/4 tsp. Ono Hawaiian Seasoning
1/2 Tbsp. fresh dill (or 1/4 tsp. dried dill)
pepper to taste

Lomi above ingredients with your hands in a large bowl. Enjoy! Will keep up to one week refrigerated in a well-sealed container.

David M. Pellegrin
Chairman/President

Maui Office:
Kihei Commercial Center
300 Ohukai Road, Unit C-315
Kihei, Hawaii 96753
(808) 875-4886, FAX (808) 874-6827

Kauai Office:
P.O. Box 3246
Lihue, Hawaii 96766
(808) 245-8910
FAX (808) 245-6419

Island of Hawaii Office:
P.O. Box 877
Hilo, Hawaii 96721
(808) 935-9822
FAX: (808) 935-5052

Dear REHAB,

PERRY: It's Perry on the LEFT...
PRICE: and Price on the RIGHT...
PERRY: and a great recipe for our friends at REHAB!
PRICE: Something my dear grandmother used to prepare.
PERRY: The recipe is for Teriyaki Burgers. Your grandmother was Portuguese.
PRICE: Teriyaki IS Portuguese! Vasco de Gama took some to Japan and they loved it. Same as sushi.
PERRY: It sounds like revised history.
PRICE: I went to Roosevelt.
PERRY: Ah...folks...enjoy the recipe.

Portuguese Teriyaki Burgers

1 1/2 pounds lean ground beef
1 1/2 cups soft bread crumbs
1/2 cup chopped onion
2 eggs, slightly beaten
1/2 cup sugar
2/3 cup soy sauce
1/3 cup water
1 teaspoon salt
2 teaspoons ginger juice
1 clove garlic, crushed

Combine beef, bread crumbs, onion and eggs.
Make sauce from remaining ingredients.
Mix 1/2 cup of sauce into meat mixture.
Form into patties and marinate in remaining sauce for 1 hour.
Broil in oven or grill on the hibachi (also a Portuguese invention).

Michael W. Perry
On the Left

Larry Price
On the Right

1505 Dillingham Boulevard, Suite 208 / Honolulu, Hawaii 96817
Phone (808) 841-8300 / Sales FAX (808) 841-9211 / News FAX (808) 841-9259

TITLE GUARANTY ESCROW SERVICES, INC.
235 Queen Street, First Floor
Honolulu, Hawaii 96813
Phone: (808) 521-0211
Fax: (808) 521-0280

Being health conscious is a family way of life. Lots of vegetables, more fruits and grains, but there's always room for dessert! My children, Bonnie, Molly, and David chose this recipe as their "favorite". It's easy to make, and healthy, too!

APPLE CRISP

4 cups peeled, sliced Apples
1/4 cup Water
4 tsp. firmly packed Brown Sugar
2 tsp. Lemon Juice
1 tsp. Cinnamon
1 cup Blueberries or Raspberries
1/2 cup Oats (Quick or Old-fashioned)
1 Tbsp. firmly packed Brown Sugar
1 Tbsp. soft Margarine

Preheat oven to 375 degrees. Combine first six ingredients and mix well. Arrange apple mixture in an 8" x 8" baking dish that has been sprayed with non-stick coating. Combine the remaining ingredients and sprinkle over apples. Bake for 30 minutes or until apples are tender and topping is slightly browned.

Yield: 8 servings

David T. Pietsch, Jr., President

TITLE GUARANTY OF HAWAII
INCORPORATED
235 QUEEN STREET • P.O. BOX 3084 • HONOLULU, HAWAII 96802 • TELEPHONE 533-6261

ONO COLESLAW

1 package saimin noodles, uncooked
(save soup base powder)

Salad:
2 Tbsp. butter
1/2 cup slivered almonds
1/2 cup sunflower seeds
1 head cabbage, shredded
6 green onions, chopped

Dressing:
Soup base (from saimin package)
1/2 cup vegetable oil
3 Tbsp. vinegar
1 Tbsp. sugar
Pepper to taste

Melt butter; toast almonds and sunflower seeds. Combine dressing ingredients. Combine all salad ingredients with dressing. Toss. Crumble raw saimin noodles and add to cabbage salad.

A potluck favorite!

MICHAEL A. PIETSCH
PRESIDENT

GECC Financial

David J. Porteus
President

GECC Financial Corporation
A unit of General Electric Capital Corporation
700 Bishop Street, Suite 1600
Honolulu, Hawaii 96813
808 527-8220

Recently, the associates of GECC Financial Corporation compiled a Cookbook to commemorate our 15th year anniversary as part of the General Electric Company. One recipe that everyone agrees is easy to prepare and delicious is "Big Al's Famous Eat'um While Its Hot" chili.

BIG AL'S CHILI

Brown together:

1 lb. hamburger*
1 medium onion
2 packages - Portuguese sausages*

* add more if you like

Add to hamburger mixture:

1 tsp. salt
1 tsp. pepper
1 Tbsp. chili powder
2-28 oz. cans whole tomatoes, drained and coarsely chopped
2-15 oz. cans chili beans
1-15 oz. can small red beans (drained)
1-8 oz. can tomato sauce

Simmer mixture uncovered for 2 hours and enjoy!

David J. Porteus

DFS
(Dad's Favorite Sauce)

Bolognese Sauce

2 lbs.	Ground Beef
1 lb. or 2 pcs.	Country Style Pork Ribs (trim off fat)
1 Medium	Maui onion, finely diced
1 Medium	Carrot, finely diced
2 Stalks	Celery, finely diced
1/4 - 1/2 tsp.	Nutmeg
1/4 - 1/2 tsp.	Sugar
1 Tbsp.	Olive Oil
1 Cup	Milk
1 Cup	Dry White Wine
2 Cans (28 oz. each)	Italian Plum Tomatoes, chopped
2 Cans (6 oz. each)	Tomato Paste
3 Pieces	Bay Leaf
	Salt & Black Pepper
	Grated Romano Cheese

1. Boil the pork ribs gently and drain. Remove from bone and shred. Set aside.

2. In a large pan, sauté onion in olive oil until pale golden brown; add celery, carrots and sauté until soft.

3. Add ground beef, large pinch of salt and black pepper. Cook until almost brown. Drain off fat. Add milk and simmer 5 minutes. Add nutmeg and sugar.

4. Raise heat to medium, and add wine. When bubbly, add tomatoes (with the liquid) and add the cooked pork ribs. Turn down heat to simmer. Add bay leaves.

5. Cook for at least 45 minutes (3 hours is best) gradually adding tomato paste to desired consistency of sauce. Add water if needed.

Let stand at least 30 minutes before serving (best if served reheated the next day). Serve atop a hearty pasta such as rigatoni, fusilli or ziti, with grated cheese.

Bon Appetit!

John L. Reed
President

DFS Hawaii
A Division of DFS Group L.P.

P.O. Box 29500
Honolulu, Hawaii
96820

Telephone: 808 837-3000
Fax: 808 837-3563 Administration
Fax: 808 837-3550 Accounting
Fax: 808 837-3433 Merchandising

Girl Scout
Council of Hawaii
420 Wyllie Street
Honolulu, Hawaii 96817
Telephone: (808) 595-8400
Facsimile: (808) 595-3006

SOME - MORES
(AKA: S'MORES)

serves 1

Here's a traditional Girl Scout Campfire favorite, our Girl Scout Alumnae had them at an event at Washington Place...go ahead, enjoy a Scouting memory!

4 squares Hershey's chocolate
2 graham crackers (1 large broken in halves)
1 marshmallow

Toast a marshmallow slowly over coals until brown, or for city slickers, microwave marshmallow 30 seconds on high. Put chocolate on graham cracker, then the toasted (or zapped) marshmallow on top, then another graham cracker. Press gently together, wait about 1 minute (if you can!) for chocolate to melt a bit and eat. Makes you want "some more"!

JOYCE RICHARDS
Executive Director

Girl Scout Council Service Centers
KAUAI: 4268 I Rice St., Lihue, HI 96766 (808) 245-4984/FAX 246-9285
MAUI: 200 Liholiho Street, Wailuku, HI 96793 (808) 244-3744/FAX 244-4747
HAWAII: P.O. Box 934, Keaau, HI 96749 (808) 966-9376/FAX (808) 966-8452
and 74-5543 Kaiwi Street #G, Kailua-Kona, HI 96740 (808) 329-5101/FAX 329-7291

A United Way Agency

Old Glory by John Perio — Pastels, 1994

"While the excellent care from doctors, nurses and therapists helped to heal his body, the afternoon John discovered REHAB's Louis Vuitton Creative Arts Program, his SPIRIT began to heal."

—by Susan Perio (wife)

GARY W. RODRIGUES
State Director, UPW
President, Hawaii AFL-CIO
Judicial Panel, AFSCME

GARY'S WALNUT PIE

3/4	cup sugar
1/4	cup all-purpose flour
1/4	tsp. salt
1/2	cup milk
3	eggs
1 1/4	cup dark corn syrup
6	tbsp. (3/4 stick) unsalted butter, melted
3/4	tsp. vanilla extract
1	cup walnuts (4 oz.), coarsely chopped
1	unbaked 9-inch pie crust

Preheat oven to 350 degrees.

Mix together sugar, flour and salt in medium size bowl. Stir in milk until smooth. Add eggs, corn syrup, butter and vanilla extract until thoroughly blended.

Scatter walnuts over bottom of pie crust. Pour in egg mixture.

Bake at 350 degrees for 1 hour, or until top is puffed and browned. Cool pie on wire rack to room temperature. Refrigerate for 2 hours. Top with whipped cream if you wish.

Gary W. Rodrigues
State Director

Longs Drug Stores

Hawaii District Office: 2270 Hoonee Place, Honolulu, Hawaii 96819

Easy to make and deliciously elegant for entertaining when served on a silver platter.

BAKED SALMON WITH VERMOUTH

2 lbs. salmon fillet
garlic salt
1/4 cup butter
1/2 cup fresh mushrooms, sliced
1/2 cup Maui onions, thinly sliced
2 Tbsp. capers
1/4 cup Vermouth

Sprinkle garlic salt on both sides of fillet and place fish on a sheet of foil. Saute sliced mushrooms and onions in butter and pour over salmon. Sprinkle with capers and pour Vermouth over salmon. Secure foil and bake in preheated oven at 350 degrees for 20-25 minutes.

Gerald H. Saito
Vice President and
Hawaii District Manager

Kenneth H. Sandefur
Area Vice President

Suite 400
One Waterfront Plaza
Honolulu, Hawaii 96813

For a person who loves Italian food, I have found this recipe to be a great tasting dish. I have also found it to be a very easy one to prepare.

Crusty sour dough bread is a nice accompaniment

Pasta with Sausages and Cream Sauce

- 1/2 pound sweet, regular, or hot Italian sausage
- 1 1/2 tablespoons chopped onion
- 2 tablespoons butter
- 1/2 tablespoon extra virgin olive oil
- 2/3 cup heavy whipping cream
- Black pepper, ground fresh
- Salt
- 1 pound pasta
- Freshly grated parmigiano - reggiano cheese at the table

Recommended pasta: It is perfect sauce for those shapes of pasta whose twists or cavities can trap little morsels of sausage and cream. Conchiglie, fusilli, and penne are the best examples.

1. Skin the sausage and crumble it as fine as possible
2. Put the chopped onion, butter and olive oil in a small saucepan, turn the heat on to medium, and cook until the onion becomes colored a pale gold. Add the crumbled sausage and cook for 10 minutes. Add a few grindings of pepper (to taste) and all the cream, turn the heat up to medium high, and cook until the cream has thickened, stirring once or twice. Taste and correct for salt.
3. Toss the sauce with cooked drained pasta and serve at once with grated parmesan on the side.

Ken Sandefur

Kenneth H. Sandefur

MAUI LAND & PINEAPPLE COMPANY, INC.

MANGO (OR PINEAPPLE) CHUTNEY

4 quarts (25 cups) green mangoes or pineapple, peeled and sliced

4 cups sugar

3 cups cider vinegar

3 onions, chopped

2 Tbsp. garlic, chopped

1/2 cup fresh ginger root, chopped

1-1/2 tsp. dried red pepper, crushed

1-1/2 cup raisins

1-1/2 tsp. salt

Cook sugar and vinegar in stainless steel pot (or pots) until dissolved. Add sliced fruit. Cook at slow boil until pieces start to get soft and translucent.

Add other ingredients. Cook until chutney starts to darken and fruit is soft, but not mushy. This takes between 30 to 60 minutes, depending upon ripeness of the fruit. Do not overcook.

Sterilize jars, lids and wide-mouth funnel in boiling water. Ladle warm chutney into jars using funnel. Pour melted paraffin slowly on top of chutney. Cover immediately. When cooled, screw on lids.

Makes approximately 6 quarts of chutney. Will keep indefinitely, getting darker and eventually drier. Once opened, refrigerate.

Mary Cameron Sanford

MARY CAMERON SANFORD
Chairman of the Board

P.O. Box 187, Kahului, Hawaii 96732-0187 • (808) 877-3351 • Fax (808) 871-0953

This recipe was given to my wife years ago just before we got married. It is definitely a family favorite because it is such a delicious marinade and is so easy to make. Our children all consider it to be the best. We think you will, too.

Basic Bar-B-Q Sauce

Mix:
- 1 cup soy sauce
- 3/4 cup sugar (we use brown)
- 2 Tbsp. mirin or red wine (we use mirin)
- 1 Tbsp. vegetable oil
- Ginger and garlic -- grated or crushed

Marinate beef, chicken, pork or fish for several hours before broiling or grilling.

Variations
crushed red pepper, chopped green onions, sesame oil instead of vegetable oil, black pepper, chopped onions, Tabasco sauce

Peter B. Savio
President

HONOLULU OFFICE
931 University Avenue, #202
Honolulu, Hawaii 96826
Phone: (808) 942-7701
Fax: (808) 942-2721

RENTAL DEPARTMENT
931 University Avenue, #208
Honolulu, Hawaii 96826
Phone: (808) 942-9477
Fax: (808) 951-6505

EAST OAHU OFFICE
377 Keahole Street, #200
Honolulu, Hawaii 96825
Phone: (808) 396-9999
Fax: (808) 395-4200

AIEA OFFICE
98-199 Kamehameha Hwy. B10
Aiea, Hawaii 96701
Phone: (808) 486-5555
Fax: (808) 487-7154

LEEWARD OFFICE
94-1021 Waipahu Street
Waipahu, Hawaii 96797
Phone: (808) 671-7777
Fax: (808) 677-1404

HILO OFFICE
162 Kinoole Street, #201
Hilo, Hawaii 96720
Phone: (808) 934-7300
Fax: (808) 934-7400

PETER H. SCHALL
Managing Director
Area General Manager-Hawaii

Hilton Hawaiian Village

GRILLED CHICKEN CAESAR

Marinade:	4 pcs.	8 oz.	Chicken breasts (boneless)
	1/2	small	Onion (sliced)
	1/2	cup	Olive oil
	1	sprig	Rosemary
	1	tsp.	Dijon mustard
			Salt and Pepper (to taste)
Dressing:	1	cup	Olive oil
	2	tbsp.	Balsamic vinegar
	1/4	cup	White vinegar
	2	each	Egg yolks
	2		Whole lemons (squeeze juice)
	1	tsp.	Dijon mustard
	2	each	Anchovy filets
	2	cloves	Garlic (chopped fine)
	2	tbsp.	Parmesan cheese (grated
			Salt and Pepper (to taste)
	2	heads	Romaine lettuce
	1	cup	Toasted bread croutons or fried won ton chips

Marinate chicken breasts in olive oil mixture over night. Clean Romaine lettuce and tear leaves into bite sizes from stems. Dry leaves and refrigerate.

Dressing: In a blender, add egg yolks, mustard, garlic, anchovies, salt, pepper and half of vinegar. Slowly add oil and vinegar until it becomes a creamy texture; add lemon juice and grated parmesan cheese.

Broil or saute both sides of chicken breasts in hot pan for five minutes; cut into 1/2" strips.

Place Romaine lettuce in bowl for family style or on individual plates. Put warm chicken strips on top and add bread croutons or won ton chips. Add Caesar dressing (about 2 tbsp. per person). Add more grated parmesan cheese if desired. For family style, toss all ingredients in bowl together and serve warm.

Peter H. Schall

2005 Kalia Road, Honolulu, Hawaii 96815-1999 Telephone 808-949-4321 Telex 8380
Reservations 1-800-HILTONS

FLAN DE LECHE

(Creme Caramel)

You will need:
- 2 cups milk
- 6 eggs
- 3/4 cup sugar
- 1 Tbsp. vanilla
- 1 stick cinnamon
- 5 pieces lime peel

Caramel:
- 10 Tbsp. sugar

Boil milk, cinnamon and lime peels. Add sugar slowly, stir, make sure milk doesn't over-boil or burn.

Let the milk cool for 15 minutes. Remove cinnamon stick and lime peels. Beat eggs, add to the cool milk together with vanilla.

Mix all ingredients and pour into mold already with caramel in it.

How to make caramel: Turn stove to high heat. Put 10 Tbsp. of sugar in a small pan. Dissolve, tilting back and forth. Pour liquid in mold before you add the milk mixture.

Fill large baking pan with water. Put mold in the middle and bake in 275 degree oven for one hour or until wooden pick inserted in center comes out clean. Cool thoroughly. Loosen sides with spatula and invert flan over serving dish.

Enjoy!

Richard F. Schaller
General Manager

1290 Ala Moana Blvd. • Honolulu, HI 96814-4299 • 808-593-4444 • FAX 808-593-9446
HONOLULU 4 • Maui 12 • Hilo 13

REHAB *Rebuilding Lives Together*

Rehabilitation Hospital of the Pacific • 226 North Kuakini Street • Honolulu, HI 96817 • Telephone: (808) 531-3511 • FAX: 544-3335

This recipe first came to our family via a little cookbook put together for Mother's Day in one of our children's Punahou classes back in the late sixties. It quickly became a family favorite and our thirty-five year old son still requests it when he comes home for a visit. It's quick, easy, economical and delicious! Ole!!!

PEDRO'S SPECIAL

1 tablespoon (or less) vegetable oil
1 lb. ground beef, extra lean is fine
1 chopped medium onion
1 clove garlic minced
1 can (14 1/2 oz.) diced tomatoes in juice
1/4 teaspoon oregano
2 tablespoons chili powder
1 lb. can kidney beans with liquid
1 medium bag Fritos corn chips

Brown the meat, onion, and garlic in the oil. Stir in the tomatoes, oregano, and the chili powder, simmer for five minutes Grease a casserole dish and alternate meat mixture with the beans and corn chips (it should make two layers of each), ending with the chips. Bake it covered for 35 minutes at 350 degrees. Uncover and bake an additional 10 minutes.

Toppings
Shredded lettuce
Chopped green onion
Grated cheddar cheese
Chopped black olives
Chopped green onions
Sour cream

Before serving top with any or all of the above ingredients. Serves four generously.

Patricia T. Schnack

PUNAHOU 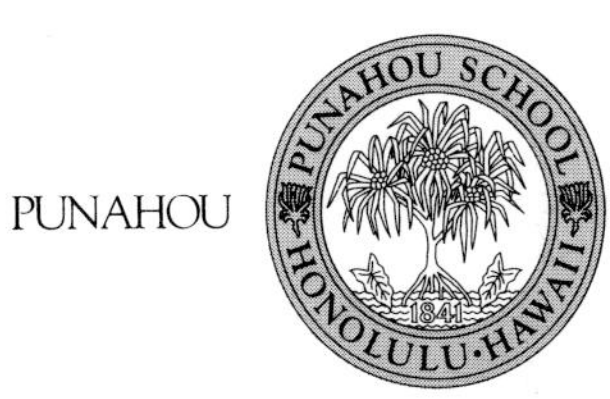 SCHOOL • 1601 PUNAHOU STREET • HONOLULU, HI 96822 • PH: (808) 944-5700 • FAX: (808) 944-5779

James K. Scott
President

PUNAHOU CARAMEL CUTS

(Punahou's favorite for the past 50 years!)

1 Cup butter or margarine
2 Cups flour
3 1/2 Cups brown sugar
1 1/4 teaspoons vanilla
1 1/2 teaspoons baking powder
3 eggs
3/4 cups chopped nuts (optional)

Melt the butter in a saucepan to the boiling point. Pour the butter over the brown sugar in a mixing bowl and blend. While warm, add the eggs and vanilla. Add the dry ingredients and nuts.

Pour the batter into a cookie pan (17 1/4 x 11 1/2 x 1" works well). Bake at 350 degrees for 30 minutes. Cut into squares, using a plastic knife for easier cutting.

Jim Scott
President
Punahou School

HAWAII STEVEDORES, INC.

P.O. Box 2160 • Honolulu, Hawaii 96805-2160 • Phone (808) 527-3400

CHINESE STYLE CHICKEN

4-5 lbs. chicken thigh

Sauce

3/4 cup shoyu
3/4 cup water
I inch piece ginger, crushed fine
I clove garlic, crushed
I/4 cup brown sugar
I whole five star flower
3 Tbsp. honey

6 stalks green onion, chopped

Simmer sauce I5 minutes (except onions). Add chicken and simmer additional 45 minutes. Add green onions. Thicken with I/4 cup corn starch with water.

Serve on a bed of blanched broccoli. Delicious!

GEORGE Y. SERIKAKU
PRESIDENT

CONTRACT STEVEDORES • TERMINAL SERVICES • EQUIPMENT MAINTENANCE

SHELTON CORPORATION
900 ALA MOANA BOULEVARD
HONOLULU, HAWAII 96814
PHONE (808) 599-3805 FAX (808) 521-7010

This is a recipe passed down to me from my mother, from her mother and so on... My wife, Lesley, grows fresh mint in our gardens. It's a wonderful sauce to be used over any type of meat you would normally want mint jelly on.

ENGLISH MINT SAUCE

1 cup of firmly packed fresh mint leaves (remove stalks!)

Chop leaves finely (they chop easier if leaves are damp)

Place chopped leaves in bottom of your pouring container and sprinkle just enough white sugar over them to cover.

Pour about 1/5 - 1/4 cup BOILING water in the container to dissolve sugar. BOILING water is a must, it helps to retain the rich green color.

Add 3/4 cup vinegar (white or malt, whichever is your taste preference)

This should make enough to serve 4 to 6 people.

Tony Shelly

Anthony L. Shelly
President

HERE'S A RECIPE THAT IS SO FABULOUS, IT IS EVEN DEVOURED BY SMALL CHILDREN, IN FACT CHILDREN OF ALL SIZES, IN SPITE OF THE FACT THAT IT CONTAINS THE DREADED " S " INGREDIENT---
" SPINACH " !!!

THIS IS A GREAT PUPU, SIDE DISH OR ANY KIND OF DISH!!

SPINACH APPETIZER

1 small onion finely chopped
2 beaten eggs (at room temp is best)
1 10oz. box of cooked/ drained frozen
chopped spinach (1 cup)
1/2 stick to 1 full stick room temp margarine
(to taste, but I prefer 1/2 stick)
1 cup milk
1 cup flour
1 lb. cubed Monterey Jack cheese
1 tsp. salt
1 tsp. baking powder
1/2 cup parmesan cheese
sprinkle of garlic

Mix all ingredients together, then fold in both cheeses.
Pour into a 9 x 13 pan and bake at 350 degrees for 45 minutes.

Let stand for 10 minutes before cutting.
Don't eat the whole pan alone!!

SAM SHENKUS

Property Management Office
101 Ala Moana Boulevard
Suite 3000
Honolulu, Hawaii 96813
Telephone: 808-528-5700
Fax: 808-524-8334

1210 Ward Avenue
Honolulu, Hawaii 96814-1488
Telephone 808 536-3808

Vladimir Ossipoff, FAIA
Sidney E. Snyder, AIA
Alan Rowland, AIA

Wade Y. Terao, AIA

Ossipoff, Snyder & Rowland Architects

TONIGHT SOUP

This can make a meal for 4-6 or be a substantial first course for 8. The taste is of fresh vegetables with a meat broth. The only fat is from butter and the meat, and this is under 50 caolories per serving.

Cooking begins with the meat/shoyu/salt/onion and butter. Continue by chopping and adding vegetable ingredients. The 1/8" and 1/4" thickness allows fast cooking and tasteful results.

I invented this by using available ingredients.

In a heavy 4 quart pot or pan at medium high heat add the following, and cook by tossing and lightly browning meat and onions.

1/2 tsp. garlic salt
1/2 tsp. shoyu light
2 hot dog weiners - lo fat type, cut in 1/8" thick slices.
1 medium to large onion chopped 1/8" thick slices.
2 bay leaves
6 stalks celery - 1/8" thick slices
12 stalks asparagus - 1/4" thick slices
1 tbs. butter
2 medium potatoes sliced to 1/8" thickness, then chopped
2 carrots - split lengthwise, chopped 1/8" thick
1 cup frozen green beans (fresh ok), chopped to 1/2" pieces
1 can (14-1/2 ounces) fat free chicken broth
3-5 cups water to taste

Start cooking meat, then chop and add other ingredients. This may take 15 minutes. Add water and broth, cook for 20-30 minutes or until potatoes are cooked through.

In just over one-half hour you have soup, with lots of fresh vegetable flavor and a meat broth.

Salt/garlic/shoyu/pepper to taste and serve.

Sidney E. Snyder, Jr., AIA
President

Merchandise Group

Hawaii District Offices
98-600 KAMEHAMEHA HIGHWAY
PEARL CITY, HAWAII 96782

ELTON T. TANAKA
District Manager

PERSIMMON COOKIES

1 cup sugar
1/2 cup butter

2 cups flour
1 cup chopped nuts
1 cup raisins
1/2 tsp. cloves
1/2 tsp. cinnamon
1/2 tsp. nutmeg

* 1 cup persimmon pulp
1 tsp. baking soda
1 egg

Cream butter and sugar.

Add nuts, raisins, cloves, cinnamon and nutmeg to the flour.

Mix persimmon pulp with baking soda.
Beat egg and add to persimmon mixture.

Then add the flour mixture to the persimmon mixture.

Drop 1 teaspoon at a time on an ungreased cookie sheet.
Bake 350° approximately 10 minutes or until golden brown.
Yield: 4 dozen

* Remove skin and seeds of 3-4 medium persimmons then osterize to pulp stage.

Elton Tanaka

A SEARS ROEBUCK COMPANY

Below is a recipe remarkably deceiving. It looks too simple to be sooooo good. But truly, it is easy to make and wonderful to eat. For you chocolate lovers, once you try it, it will become a regular around the house!

GRANNY'S CHOCOLATE CAKE

1 Chocolate Cake Mix

1 Chocolate Instant Pudding (small)

1 Package Chocolate Chips

2 Eggs

1 3/4 Cup Milk

Mix all ingredients and pour into greased bundt pan.
Cook at 350° for 1 hour.

Jon Thomas

letjt03.doc/m38

770 Kapiolani Boulevard, Suite 100, Honolulu, HI 96813 (808) 547-4176

the art of chocolate
supplies • classes • special occasions

Carol Tominaga
General Partner

OYSTER SAUCE CHICKEN

1 whole chicken fryer
1/2 cup oyster sauce
1 can chicken broth
9 pieces *shiitake*, sliced
Pepper, to taste
2 Tsp Hawaiian salt
1 can bamboo shoots, sliced
1/2 cup green onions, chopped
Salt, to taste
Cornstarch

Rub chicken generously with oyster sauce and Hawaiian salt. Bake at 450 degrees for the first 15 minutes. Bring oven temperature down to 375 degrees for the next hour. Shred chicken on large platter, cover with bamboo shoots, *shiitake,* green onions.

Gravy: Bring chicken broth to boil, add cornstarch and water to thicken. Add salt and pepper to taste.

Carol Tominaga

manoa square
2961 e manoa road • honolulu, hawaii 96822
(808) 988-2585

F.E. TROTTER, INC
1100 Alakea Street, Suite 1204, Honolulu, Hawaii 96813
Telephone (808) 523-9270 • Fax (808) 523-9272

As a long-time director of The Rehabilitation Hospital of the Pacific, I have always been involved with their fundraising efforts and I am pleased to be included in this one as well.

This recipe is fancy enough for company and easy enough for just the family on work days.

Glazed Corned Beef and Pears

4 lbs. corned beef
6 whole cloves
1 can Bartlett pear halves
1/2 cup brown sugar
1 tsp. grated orange peel
1/3 cup sauterne
1 tsp. grated lemon peel
1/2 tsp. dry mustard

Cover corned beef with hot water and simmer one hour per pound.

Remove corned beef and place on platter and score fat on top in diamond pattern and stud with cloves. Drain pears, reserving one-half cup pear syrup.

Combine reserved pear syrup, brown sugar, sauterne, lemon and orange peels, and dry mustard.

Bake corned beef at 350 for 30 minutes, brushing frequently with the glaze.

Place pears around corned beef and brush with the glaze and continue to bake an additional ten minutes. (You may want to double the glaze.)

Fred E. Trotter

Fred E. Trotter

Tony S. Vericella
Regional Vice President
and General Manager

This is an original recipe by my wife, Dana. It's easy to prepare and a favorite with my children and guests. We hope you enjoy it as much as we do.

"DIRT"

INGREDIENTS

1 Stick Margarine (Melted & Cooled)

1 8 oz. Cream Cheese

1 Cup Powdered Sugar

2 Small Boxes French Vanilla Pudding (Instant)

2 1/2 Cups Milk

20 ounces Cool Whip

1 Large Package Oreo Cookies (crushed)

Using an electric mixer, combine margarine, cream cheese and powdered sugar. Mix separately pudding, milk and Cool Whip, then add to margarine combination. In large bowl, layer oreos then pudding mixture (alternating, approximately four layers). Chill for a few hours and serve.

Hawaii Region

Budget
Rent a Car
Systems, Inc.

P.O. Box
15188

Honolulu, HI
96830-0188

Phone:
808/599-2221

Fax:
808/599-2220

HAWAII PRINCE HOTEL

WAIKIKI

Roasted Rack of Veal
with Basil Mashed Potatoes and Baby Carrots

Serves 4

Ingredients

2½ - 3½ lb. Rack of Veal (If not available use lamb rack)

For the Crust:

½ cup	Panko
½ cup	Crumbled Cornbread
1 Tbsp.	Chopped Garlic
2 Tbsp.	Chopped Fresh Herbs (Basil, Thyme, Parsley)
1 Tbsp.	Chopped Green Peppercorn
1 Tbsp.	Spice Mix (Paprika, Thyme, Pepper, Chili Powder, Coriander, Salt, Cayenne Pepper and Cumin in equal parts)

Mix all ingredients well

2 Tbsp. Dijon Mustard - keep aside

Procedure

1. Season meat well and brown in a large pan or skillet. Cook at 375° for 35-45 minutes, on the middle rack of the oven.

2. When meat is almost done (when 2/3 of the required cooking time has passed) brush it generously with Dijon mustard and bread it with crust mixture (let the meat cool for a few minutes before doing, it will be easier to handle). Finish in the oven until breading is browned.

3. Place two large tablespoons of the mashed potatoes in the center of the plate. Cut your rack that has rested for at least 10 minutes into 4 equal pieces. Lean meat against potato (bone sticking up), garnish with baby carrots and if you have homemade chutney and a leaf of nice green basil.

Chris von Imhof
President and General Manager

Hawaii Prince Hotel, 100 Holomoana, Honolulu, Hawaii 96815 Telephone: (808) 956-1111 Facsimile: (808) 946-0811

PRINCE HOTELS

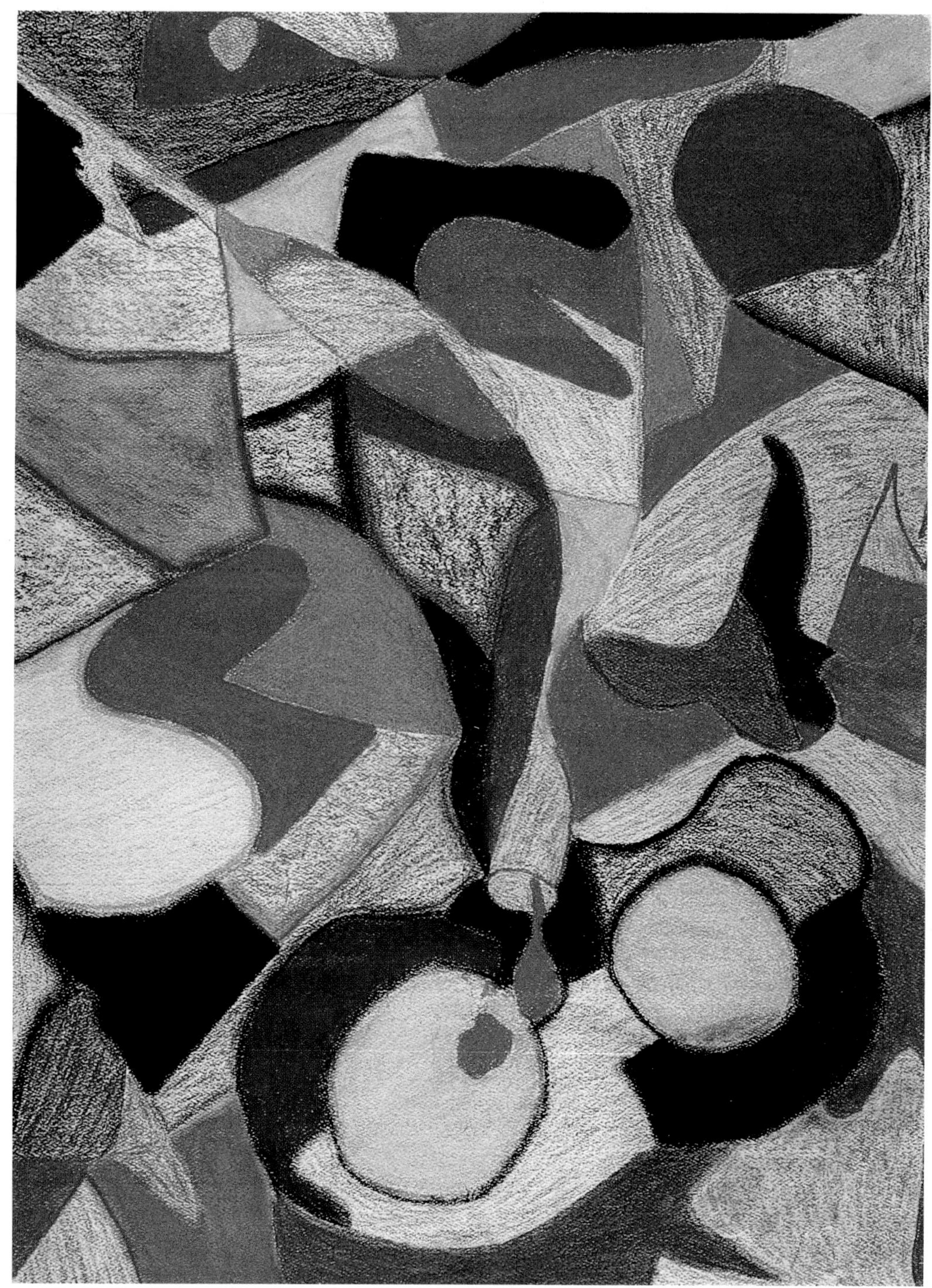

Tabasco and Eggs by Riva LaVoy *Pastels, 1994*

"Art is HOT!"

WATANABE, ING & KAWASHIMA
ATTORNEYS AT LAW
A PARTNERSHIP INCLUDING LAW CORPORATIONS
HAWAII TOWER, 5th & 6th FLOORS
745 FORT STREET
HONOLULU, HAWAII 96813

TELEPHONE (808) 544-8300
FACSIMILE: (808) 544-8399

Jan M. L. Y. Amii
George B. Apter
John R. Aube
Michael C. Bird
Peter L. Fritz
Beth K. Fujimoto
William H. Gilardy, Jr.
Lyle Y. Harada
Brian Y. Hiyane
Dennis J. Hwang
J. Douglas Ing
Donna Y. Kanemaru
James Kawashima
Curtis C. Kim
Patsy H. Kirio
John T. Komeiji
Teri Y. Kondo
Wray H. Kondo
Pamela J. Larson
Ronald Y. K. Leong
Michael A. Lorusso
Jeff N. Miyashiro
Lani Narikiyo
Kevin H. Oda
Elena J. Onaga
Seth M. Reiss
John S. Sasaki
Marcus B. Sierra
Robert T. Takamatsu
Gregory Y. P. Tom
Jeffrey N. Watanabe
Cynthia Winegar
Randall Y. Yamamoto
Lloyd S. Yoshioka

OF COUNSEL:
George R. Ariyoshi
ASIA PACIFIC CONSULTANT:
Dr. Victor Hao Li
GOVERNMENT AFFAIRS ADVISOR:
Millicent M.Y.H. Kim
PRACTICE GROUPS:
Asia Pacific Consulting Group
Banking and Real Estate Group
Commercial Litigation Group
Construction Management & Professional Design Group
Corporate, Commercial & Finance Group
Government & Regulatory Affairs Group
Insurance Defense Litigation Group
Labor, Employment & Employee Benefits Group
Land Use & Environmental Group
Legislative Affairs Group
Non-Profits Group

Antipasto Recipe

Roasted Peppers and Anchovies

12-15 fresh red bell peppers
3 to 4 cans anchovy fillets
1/2 cup chopped parsley
1/2 lb. bay shrimp
Basalmic Vinegar
Extra Virgin Olive Oil

Wash and roast peppers under broiler until black, turning to roast all sides. Place in plastic bag until cool. Skin will peel off easily. Remove white strings and seeds from inside peppers. Separate into portion size pieces and lay flat on large platter. Lay whole anchovy on each pepper piece. Sprinkle parsley and shrimp generously over platter of peppers. Drizzle with Olive Oil and Basalmic Vinegar. Serves 10 to 12.

JEFFREY N. WATANABE

CLINIC & HOSPITAL

888 South King Street
Honolulu, Hawaii 96813
(808) 522-4000

Since the Rehabilitation Hospital of the Pacific has a special place in the hearts of all of us at Straub, I am pleased to share this heart healthy meatless lasagna with our Rehab friends.

SPINACH LASAGNA

6	lasagna noodles
1/2	cup chopped onion
2	Tbsp. margarine
2	Tbsp. cornstarch
1	Tbsp. dried parsley flakes
1	tsp. dried basil, crushed
1/4	tsp. garlic powder
1/8	tsp. ground nutmeg
2	cups milk
1	10 oz. package frozen chopped spinach, thawed and drained
1	2-1/4 oz. can sliced pitted ripe olives, drained
1	3/4 cup ricotta cheese
1	beaten egg
1	8 oz. package shredded mozzarella cheese
1/2	cup grated Parmesan cheese

(Low fat cheese, margarine, and milk can be used for low fat content)

Cook lasagna noodles in a large amount of boiling salted water for 10 to 12 minutes or until tender; drain, and rinse in cold water.

In medium saucepan cook onion in margarine until tender. Stir in cornstarch, parsley, basil, garlic powder, and nutmeg. Add milk all at once. Cook and stir until thick and bubbly. Stir in spinach and olives. Set aside.

In a bowl, stir together the ricotta cheese and egg. Add mozzarella cheese and half the Parmesan cheese. Mix well. Set aside.

Arrange three noodles in the bottom of a greased 12 x 7-1/2 x 2 inch baking dish. Top with half the spinach mixture. Spoon on half of the ricotta cheese mixture. Repeat layers. Sprinkle with remaining Parmesan cheese.

Bake in oven at 350 degrees about 40 minutes or until cheese is slightly golden and mixture is bubbly. Let stand for 10 minutes.

Blake E. Waterhouse

BLAKE E. WATERHOUSE, M.D.
President/CEO

WATUMULL BROS. LTD.
P. O. BOX 3283 • HONOLULU, HAWAII 96801

Operating as:
WATUMULL'S
HAWAII FASHIONS
WAIKIKI SHOPS

The following recipe is a great favorite of not only our family but friends who come to dinner.

MUSTARD SEED POTATOES

INGREDIENTS

3 to 4 Medium Potatoes
1 Tsp. Black or Yellow Mustard Seeds
1 Tbsp. Oil
1 Small Onion (Sliced Thin)
1/2 Tsp. Turmeric Powder
3 Tbsp. Lemon Juice
1 Tbsp. Chopped Chinese Parsley or
Dry Parsley Flakes
Dash Cayenne Pepper
Salt to Taste

DIRECTIONS

Boil Potatoes till done, peel and cut into 1 inch cubes

Heat oil in pan, when heated throw in the Mustard Seeds-in 1/2 a minute they will start to pop-cover immediately with a lid or they will fly out of the pan. When they have finished popping put sliced Onions, Turmeric Cayenne Pepper and saute for a few minutes.

Put Potatoes in and mix all of the ingredients gently. Add Lemon Juice and Salt to taste. If the Potatoes are sticking to the bottom of the pan, add a couple of tablespoons of water.

Gulab Watumull

Associates, Inc.

Public Relations

Suite 2860
737 Bishop Street
Honolulu, Hawaii 96813
Telephone 808-523-8802
FAX 808-521-6141

LEMON BAR P.R. COOKIES

crust:
1 cup soft butter
dash of salt
1/2 cup powdered sugar
2 cups flour

filling:
1/4 cup flour
2 cups sugar
4 beaten eggs
6 tablespoons lemon juice

To make crust, combine butter, salt, powdered sugar and flour. Press mixture into 9" x 13" pan. Bake at 350 degrees for 15 minutes.

For filling, combine flour and sugar; mix well. Add eggs and lemon juice. Pour into slightly cooled crust. Bake at 350 degrees for 25 minutes. Cool and sprinkle with powdered sugar.

These cookies are a real sweetener for any business deal!

Sharon R. Weiner
President and CEO

Meadow Gold Dairies, Inc.
925 Cedar Street
P. O. Box 1880
Honolulu, Hawaii 96805
(808) 949-6161

THIS IS ONE OF MY FAVORITE DESSERTS AND CAN BE A GREAT SHARING EXPERIENCE. BACK IN MINNESOTA, WE WOULD RECEIVE FRESH HOME GROWN RHUBARB FROM OUR FRIEND'S LOCAL PATCH AND RETURN THE FAVOR WITH A PORTION OF THE FRESH BAKED DESSERT!

RHUBARB DESSERT

1 1/2 CUPS BUTTER

3 CUPS FLOUR

3 TBSP. SUGAR

CRUMBLE TOGETHER, PRESS INTO A 9" X 13" PAN AND BAKE FOR 10 MINUTES AT 350 DEGREES.

5 CUPS RHUBARB, CUT UP

6 EGG YOLKS, BEATEN

4 TBSP. FLOUR

1 CUP MEADOW GOLD WHIPPING CREAM

1/4 TSP. SALT

2 CUPS SUGAR

MIX TOGETHER THEN POUR MIXTURE OVER CRUST AND BAKE 1 HOUR (MAYBE LONGER) AT 350 DEGREES.

BEAT THE 6 EGG WHITES, ADD 12 TBSP. SUGAR.

SPREAD BEATEN EGG WHITES OVER MIXTURE AND BROWN IN OVEN AT 400 DEGREES.

Jay C. Wilson

JAY C. WILSON
PRESIDENT AND GENERAL MANAGER

Bojim Investments, Inc.
EXECUTIVE OFFICES • 1314 S. KING ST., SUITE 524 • HONOLULU, HI 96814 • PH. (808) 596-0558 • FAX (808) 591-9057

WO SPECIAL FRIED RICE

INGREDIENTS:

1/2 lbs Char Siu - diced 1/4" squares
3 Chinese Pork Sausage (Lop Cheong - cut diagonally 1/8" thick
1 Preserved Salted Turnip (Chung Choi) - rinse thoroughly, squeezed dry and cut 1/4" lengths
1-1/2 Cups Frozen Garden Peas and Carrots - Thawed out
3 Cups of Cooked Rice
1 Egg (large)
6 Tbsp. Oyster Sauce

INSTRUCTIONS:

1. Heat frying pan on high flame.
2. Drop in sliced lop cheong and char siu. Fry until hot.
3. Add in chung choi - let fry a little.
4. Add Rice - Fold all ingredients evenly with rice.
5. Now you're on the home stretch!
6. When the rice and ingredients are hot - add peas and carrots. Fold in, and allow to cook 4-5 minutes.
7. When all is hot, add egg (beaten) to rice. Fold egg with rice and allow egg to cook for 1-2 minutes.
8. Add oyster sauce. Fold in and allow to become hot.
9. You now have Wo Fried Rice, with ample servings for 5 adults.

ENJOY!!

James C. Wo
Chairman

CSWo & Sons, Ltd.
Corporate Office • P.O. Box 1417 • Honolulu, Hawaii 96806 • Ph: (808) 545-5966 • Fax: (808) 531-4135

One of the greatest joys is the birth of a child. However, after the birth, the health of the mother is of utmost importance. The Chinese have long known this, and have a special prescription to ensure proper healing and recovery.

NEW MOMS: Stay home for 30 days, and.....
eat lots of pig's feet!

CHINESE PIG'S FEET

1 pair	Pig's feet
3 cups	Chinese black vinegar
1 cup	Cider vinegar
1 pkg.	Chinese brown sugar
2 thumb-size	Ginger, sliced and blanched
1	Star anise
1 tsp.	Hawaiian salt

Wash pig's feet, par boil, rinse and clean off hair with razor. In large pot, add vinegars, brown sugar, anise and salt. Bring to boil and add ginger. Simmer 5-10 minutes. Add lower part of pig's feet. Bring to boil and simmer 15 minutes. Then, add rest of pig's feet. Simmer about 1 hour.

NEW DADS: Don't eat up all the pig's feet......
save some for mom!

Bub

Robert Bub Wo
President

WATERHOUSE PROPERTIES, INC.

EDWIN S. N. WONG
Chairman, President &
Chief Executive Officer

If you're hungry and want to cook something real fast that tastes good, this is it -- HOBO STEW! I ate a lot of this during my college days at Syracuse -- it's fast, simple and ono-licious!

HOBO STEW

1 Can of corn beef
1 Round onion sliced
1 Can of peas
1 Can of carrots
1 Can of tomato paste
Salt/pepper to taste
Optional -- tabasco sauce

Saute corn beef with onions on low heat. Add can of peas and carrots (use only half of the water from both cans). Add can of tomato paste and seasoning. Simmer on low heat for about 10 minutes and serve over hot rice.

Note: You may add in other vegetables you like.

Edwin S. N. Wong

670 Queen Street, Suite 200 Honolulu, Hawaii 96813 Tel: (808) 592-4800 Fax: (808) 592-4820

Continental

Continental Airlines, Inc.
Suite 1100
1600 Kapiolani Boulevard
Honolulu HI 96814

Fax 808 942 3439

Five Spice Chicken

- **5 lbs. chicken wings and drummettes***
- **5 tbs. fresh minced ginger**
- **3 tbs. fresh minced garlic**
- **3 tbs. Chinese five spice**
- **2 tbs. table salt**
- **1 package 15 oz. tapioca flour**

√ **Let chicken thaw. Marinate with fresh ginger and garlic and place in refrigerator for 4 hours or overnight if preferred.**

√ **In a small skillet, combine 3 tbs. of five spice 2 tbs. of table salt and stir over low heat for 15 minutes.**

√ **Let spice mixture cool and then empty into a small Tupperware salt shaker.**

√ **Place marinated chicken in a large container and evenly coat with tapioca flour.**

√ **Prepare skillet or wok with heated vegetable oil, Deep fry chicken to golden brown. Let chicken drain and sprinkle your five spice and salt mixture over the chicken while still warm. Serve.**

*** Note - chicken breast cut into 2 in. strips can be substituted.**

❀❀❀❀

My father-in-law, who is great cook, taught me how to prepare this delicious Chinese dish. It's absolutely fantastic and simple to fix.

Ronald Wright

RONALD L. WRIGHT

The Children's Discovery Center, like the Rehabilitation Hospital of the Pacific, relies on its many wonderful volunteers to accomplish a myriad of tasks. Our volunteers, who we affectionately call P.A.L.s (People Assisting Learning), are giving individuals who help us do many things, from stuffing envelopes to serving on our Board of Directors to assisting children with exhibits and activities.

So what is the secret of our successful volunteer program? The "end result" of happy kids, of course! Our P.A.L.s believe, as we do, that all children share the same basic needs--to be accepted, to belong, to love and be loved. If you were to ask our P.A.L.s, they would gladly share our "secret recipe" with you. We're happy to share it with you, too!

Discovery Center's Recipe for Children

1 arm load of respect
1 ton of caring
1 gigantic portion of understanding
1 colossal can of encouragement
1 bushel of patience
1 giant box of enthusiasm

Mix all ingredients together and sprinkle liberally with love.
Serve daily to children in large doses!

Loretta Yajima

Loretta Yajima
President & CEO

Executive Office ☆ 1210 Auahi Street, Suite 102 ☆ Honolulu, Hawaii 96814
Telephone 808-592-KIDS (592-5437) ☆ Facsimile 808-592-5433

GRAND PACIFIC LIFE INSURANCE, LTD.

A member of the Finance Factors Family

WADSWORTH Y. H. YEE, J.D.
President
Chief Executive Officer

STEAMED FISH ~ THE EASY WAY

Place fish in large round bowl. If fish is too large, cut fish in half and place both halves in the bowl.

Step #1: Rub fish lightly with Hawaiian salt.

Step #2: Place slices of ginger, chopped green onion and chopped dried turnip (chung choy) over and inside of fish.

Step #3: Sprinkle a teaspoon of vegetable oil and a light shower of white pepper over fish.

Step #4: Fill pot with 1-1/2 inches of water. Place bowl with fish in pot and cover. When water comes to a boil, lower heat and sprinkle some shoyu or oyster sauce over the fish. Simmer for 15 to 30 minutes, depending on size of fish.

Step #5: Before serving, sprinkle Chinese parsley over the fish for looks and taste. They tell me parsley is good for high blood pressure.

Note: The amount of ingredients you use depends on your own taste - a splash here and a dash there.

WADSWORTH YEE

1164 Bishop Street • Suite 800 • Honolulu, Hawaii 96813-2810 • Telephone: (808) 548-5101 • Facsimile: (808) 548-5122

Benjamin J. Cayetano
GOVERNOR

Lawrence Miike
DIRECTOR OF HEALTH

STATE OF HAWAII
DEPARTMENT OF HEALTH
LANAI COMMUNITY HOSPITAL
P.O. BOX 797
LANAI CITY, HAWAII 96763

HERBERT K. YIM
HOSPITAL ADMINISTRATOR

FRED HORWITZ
ACTING
DEPUTY DIRECTOR FOR HOSPITALS

From the former **"Pineapple Island"**, we bring you Miss Letty's favorite Filipino mouth watering dessert. Don't worry about the calories, just enjoy the delicious flavor. You'll be surprised with the ease of preparation for an outcome that will bring you compliments until the last slice disappears. ***So ONO-LICIOUS.***

ROYAL BIBINGKA

- 2 lbs mochi flour
- 6 eggs(scrambled lightly)
- 6 cups milk
- 2 sticks melted butter
- 4 cups sugar
- 1 Tbsp baking powder
- 1 Tbsp vanilla extract

Preheat oven to 350 degrees. Mix all ingredients well in a large mixing bowl. Pour into a well greased 9 1/2" baking pan. Bake for approximately one (1) hour. **Use the old broom straw stick test to insure the inside is cooked.**

Please, Please let it cool before you devour! Cut in squares and watch them disappear! *Aloha from Lana'i*

BREAD PUDDING

- 4 cups milk
- 1 block butter
- 1 (heaping) cup sugar
- 1 tsp. vanilla
- 13 slices bread, sliced
- 3 eggs, beaten
- 1/2 tsp. cinnamon
- raisins (optional)

Slowly heat milk, butter, sugar and vanilla until butter melts and sugar is dissolved. Place bread cubes in a 9-inch square pan. Pour mixture over bread cubes. Add beaten eggs and cinnamon and mix well. Bake at 350 degrees for 45 minutes.

Dwight L. Yoshimura
General Manager

1450 ALA MOANA BOULEVARD, #3200, HONOLULU, HAWAII 96814
(808) 946-2811 FAX (808) 946-2216
Managed by General Growth Management of Hawaii Inc.

AIRLINES

Glenn R. Zander
President and
Chief Executive Officer
P.O. Box 30028
Honolulu, Hawaii 96820
Facsimile 808 833-3100
Telephone 808 836-4204

GLENN'S GRANDMOTHER LUCAS' LEMON PUDDING CAKE

Preheat Oven 350 Degrees

4	Tbsp	Butter
1-1/3	Cups	Granulated Sugar
4		Egg Yolks (Well Beaten)
4		Egg Whites (Stiffly Beaten)
2	tsp	Grated Lemon Rind
1/4	Cup	Lemon Juice
4	Tbsp	Flour
2	Cups	Milk

Cream butter and sugar until well blended. Mix lemon juice and lemon rind with beaten egg yolks, add to butter mixture and blend. Fold in flour, stir in milk and mix well. Fold in stiffly beaten egg whites.

Pour into greased 2-quart casserole dish. Place in larger pan on oven rack. Pour hot water into larger pan, 1 inch deep.

Bake for 35-40 minutes. Serve warm or chilled.

Glenn

GLENN R. ZANDER

Recipe Index

Appetizers & Dips

Beverages

Breads

Desserts

Recipe Index *continued*

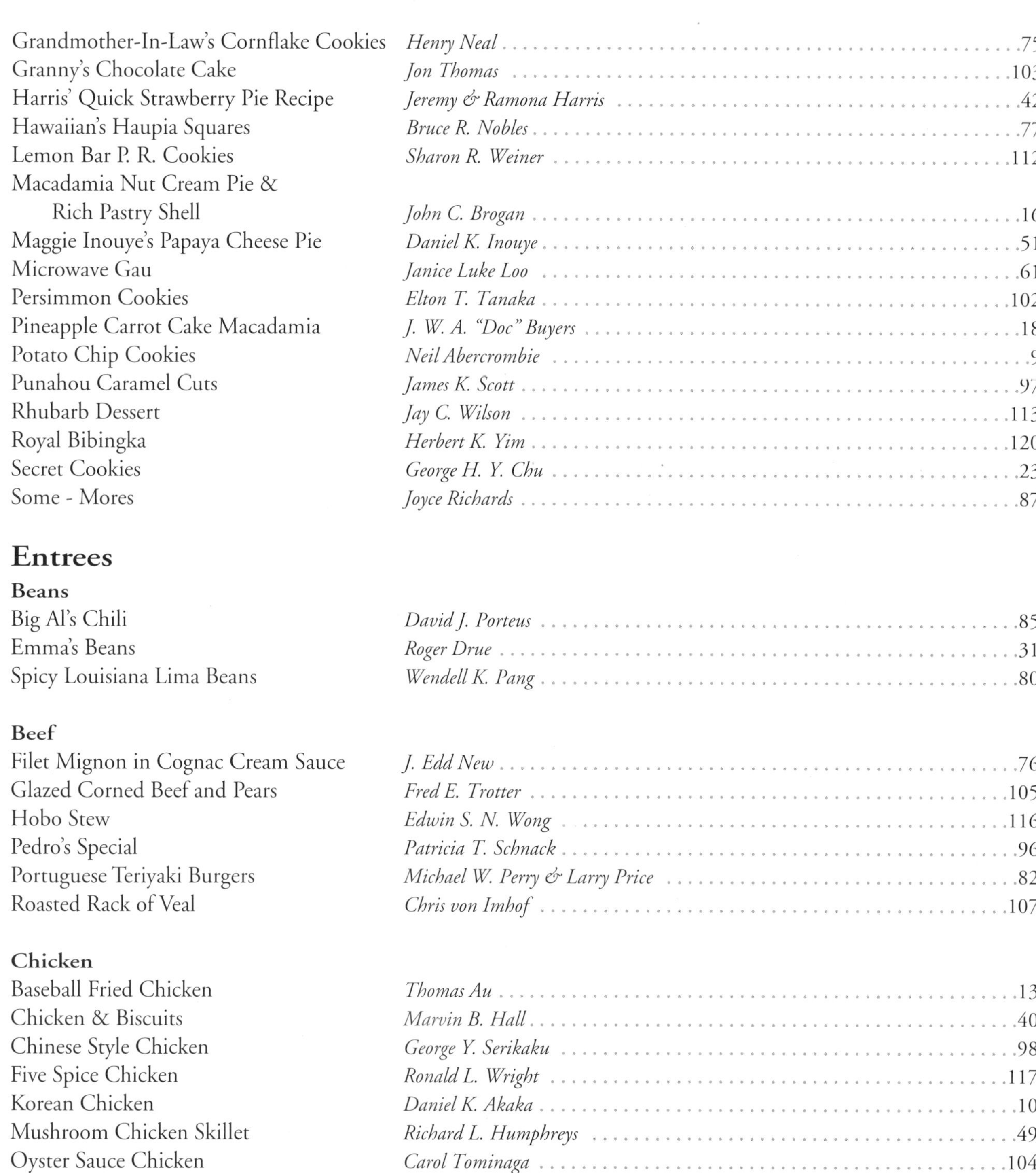

Entrees

Beans

Beef

Chicken

Recipe Index *continued*

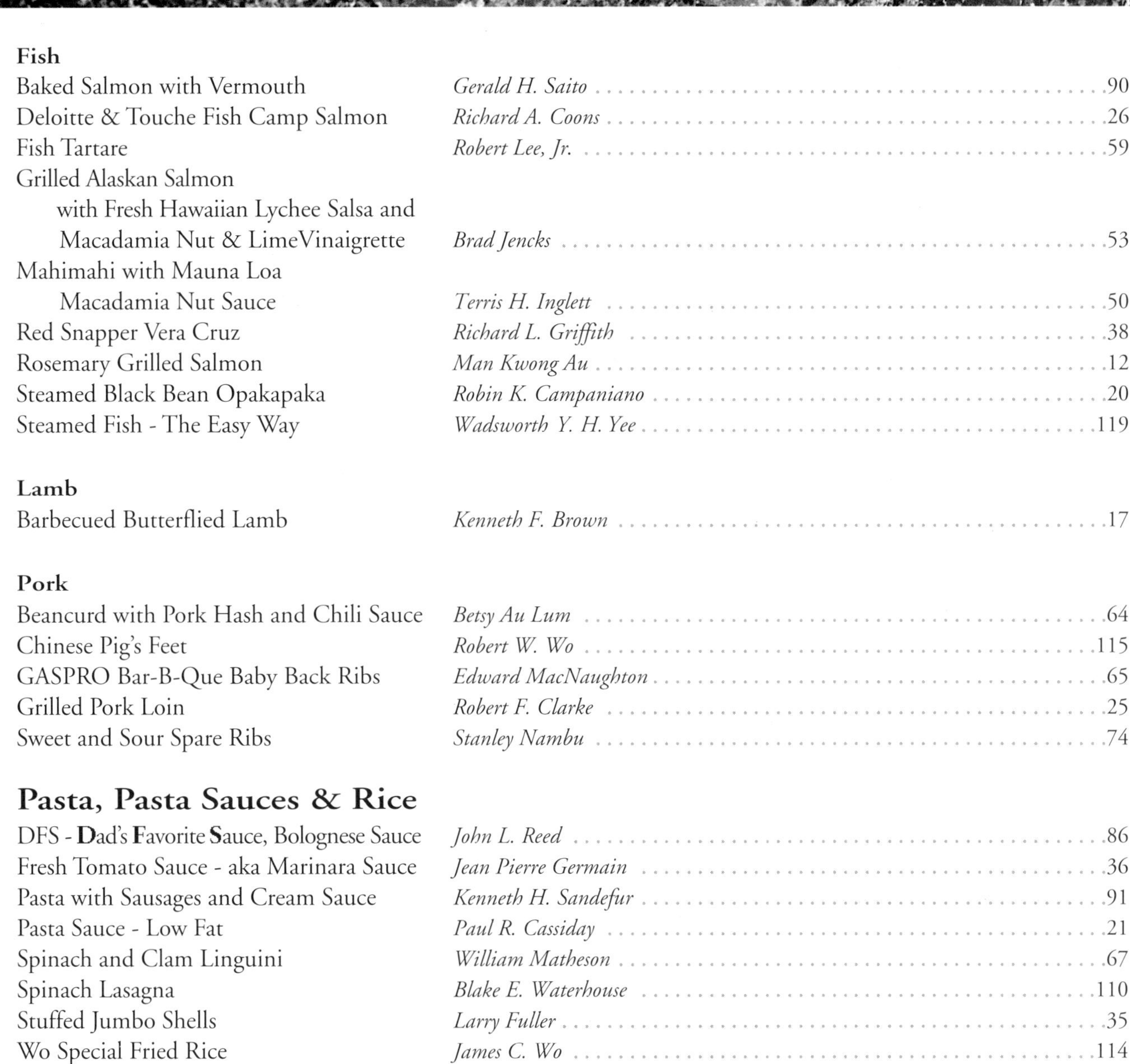

Recipe Index *continued*

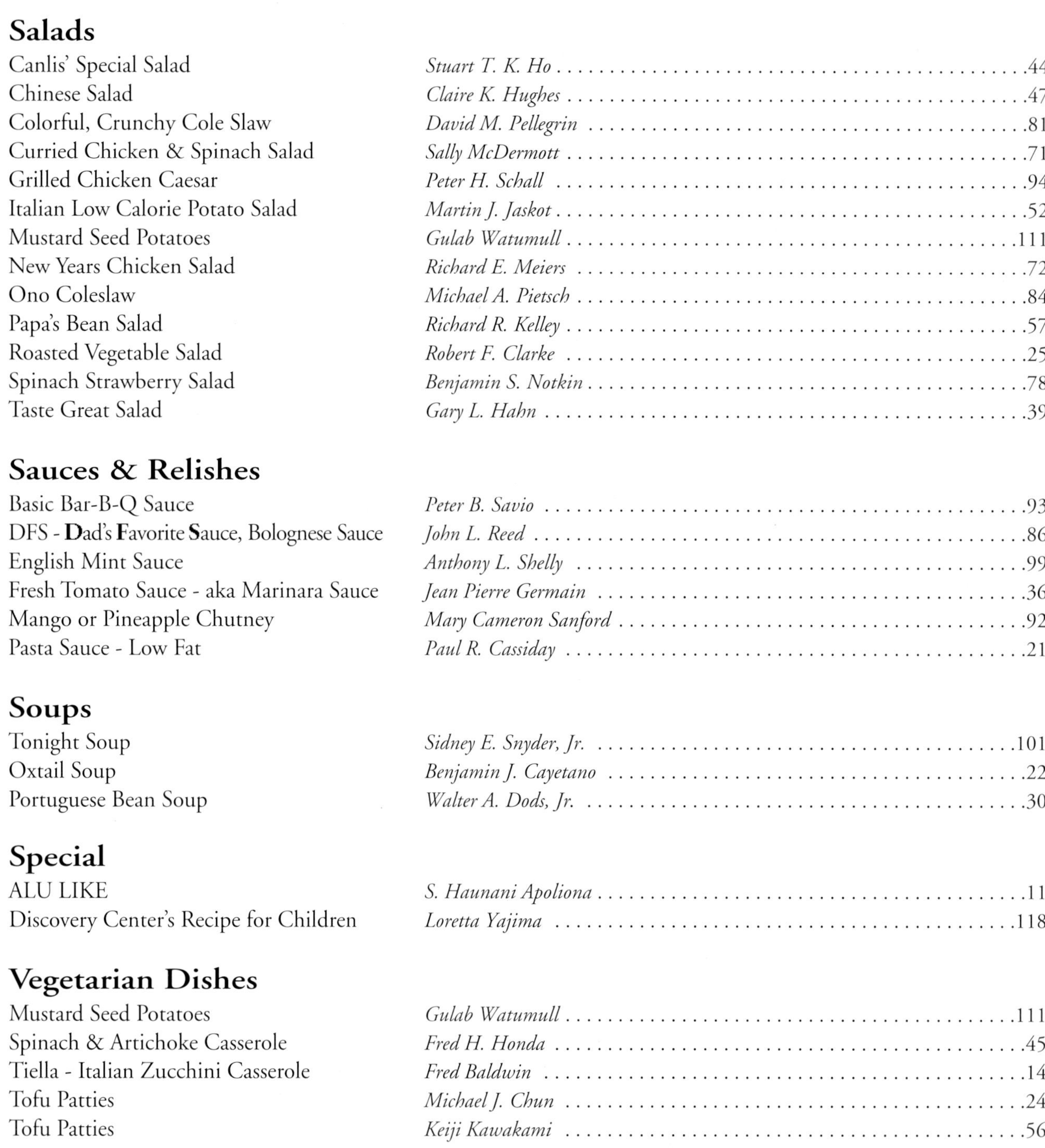

Order Form

Additional copies of THE *Taste* OF *Success,* RECIPES FROM HAWAI'I'S VIPS are available for **$19.95** per copy plus **$3.00** each for postage and handling. Copies can also be purchased directly from REHAB Hospital at 226 N. Kuakini Street, from Monday through Friday, 8:00 a.m. to 4:30 p.m. For more information, please call **(808)544-3301.**

Ordering: ________ **copies at $22.95 each = $**______________

($19.95 + $ 3.00 postage and handling)

Send to:

Name: ____

Address: ____

City: ______________ State: ________ Zip: ______________

Phone: _________________________

Method of payment: (Please do not send cash. No C.O.D. orders. Thank You.)

Check enclosed in the amount of $___________

Please make check payable to: REHAB Foundation

Please charge $ _________ to my (check one)

❑ VISA ❑ MasterCard

Card member name: _______________________________________

Card number:__________________________ Exp. date: __________

Signature:__________________________

Mail or fax order form and payment to: REHAB Foundation

226 N. Kuakini Street

Honolulu, HI 96817

Fax: (808) 544-3335

Rebuilding Lives Together

With more than 40 years of service to the people of Hawai'i and the Pacific Basin, the Rehabilitation Hospital of the Pacific (REHAB) has touched the lives of more than 65,000 individuals challenged with physical disabilities from a stroke, an injury, or other trauma. Proceeds from the sale of this cookbook will support the REHAB Hospital in order that we may continue to provide quality care.

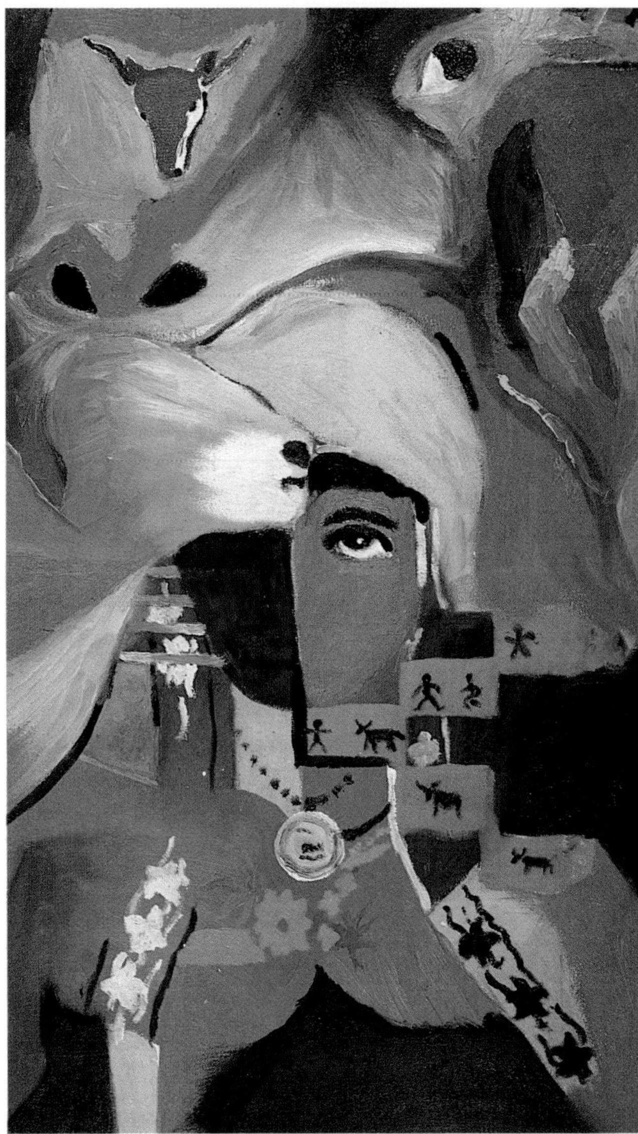

The Shepherd by Phillip Woolsey — Oil, 1995

Rehabilitation Hospital of the Pacific Foundation - Board of Directors

"REHAB's Creative Arts Program helps direct me towards a positive well being. It brings out feelings in me that I never knew I had."

The Louis Vuitton Creative Arts Program

Proceeds from the Louis Vuitton Golf Cup 1994 Hawaii Charity Tournament were donated to support REHAB's Creative Arts Program for physically challenged individuals. This program has provided a unique and creative art experience for more than 600 inpatients and 25 outpatients in 1994 alone. Throughout 1995 and 1996, works of art from this program will be on exhibit at different galleries on O'ahu and Maui.